THE ZERO DOWN BUSINESS

A Guide to Buying an Existing Business With Little to No Money

CONSTANTINE KAPOTHANASIS

Copyright © 2016 By Constantine C. Kapothanasis

202 E Main St.

Westminster, MD, 21157

(717) 409-5680

costa@kapogroup.com

All rights reserved. This book or any portion thereof may not be reproduced or used in any manner whatsoever without the express written permission of the publisher except for the use of brief quotations in a book review.

Printed in the United States of America.

Contents

ACKNOWLEDGEMENTS 1

FOREWORD 3

CHAPTER 1 INTRODUCTION 5

CHAPTER 2 Let's Get Started 24

CHAPTER 3 Let's Get into the Techniques for Buying a Business with Little to No Money 34

CHAPTER 4 Mistakes 60

CHAPTER 5 How to Read a P&L Report 70

CHAPTER 6 Conclusions 75

CHAPTER 7 Case Studies 77

ACKNOWLEDGEMENTS

This book would've never happened without the help of so many important people.

First and foremost, my undying thanks to the love of my life Caitlin with whom without none of this would be possible. The unconditional support and love from Caitlin encourages me daily to go after things that may at the time seem questionable at best. She is the only certain and unequivocal thing in my life of craziness and uncertainty, she's forever unwavering.

Thanks to my parents who gave me the tools necessary to achieve all that I have achieved up to this point in my life. I especially want to thank my Mom for instilling a self-confidence, that without I would have certainly given up a long time ago. My Mom always knew and believed I was going to be successful one day. She even knew way before everyone else, especially when most thought I wouldn't amount to much.

I want to thank all my teachers from St. Joseph's, who thought I would always turn out to be a bum.

I want to thank all of my teachers at Cheverus, who said "He doesn't apply himself." You were correct, I punted high school because I recognized very early on in the grand scheme of things that it wouldn't affect the outcome.

I want to thank all my employees, some who are twice my age, for always believing in my vision and allowing me to do the things I needed to do to turnaround some of these businesses.

I want to thank William Leonard Roberts II, for always having the type of mind that could take abstract thoughts and actions, and for having the gift of putting them into words that continuously allow individuals to truly go after their passion. He always knew the right words to give the necessary motivation to keep the engine fueled and running.

I want to thank Tayvon Jackson and Jackson Publishing for believing that my story is worth being told.

FOREWORD

There has never been a better time in history to take over an existing business that is currently making money without needing any additional money of your own to buy it. Being self-employed can be life-changing. Your quality of life can dramatically improve when you are the only person that you have to listen to.

The demographic of first generation business owners who are near retirement is incredibly high. Of this number, we have an unprecedented amount of first generation business owners with no offspring to turn their businesses over to. The highest number in our history to have no offspring or heirs.

What does this mean? It means opportunity for you. Every day thousands of businesses are closing their doors due to the inability to successfully transfer to a successor either via a sale or trade. If you have ever thought about owning your own business, then these unfortunate circumstances can become your very opportunity. I have successfully navigated the purchase of several businesses with little and sometimes ZERO money.

After I did it the first time I thought, *I'm the luckiest guy in the world.* After I did it the second time I thought, *Wow! This is like hitting the lotto.* After the third and fourth time, I realized this is a skill that can be learned and applied across many venues.

In a time where entrepreneurship has become hip, everyone is gearing towards online startups and vlogs or blogs, while seemingly overlooking a huge segment of our economy - the existing brick and mortar small businesses that make up our neighborhoods. Throughout this book, I share actionable advice with well-defined tactics that can be used to negotiate the purchase and transfer of an existing business for little and sometimes ZERO dollars.

After you conclude this book, you will efficiently know where to look for businesses that are for sale, how to successfully navigate dealing with business brokers, and finally – expertly and successfully negotiate the purchase of the business from the current owner.

If you ever thought about owning a business, then now is the time to do it, and equipped with the strategies provided in *"The Zero Down Business,"* I have no doubt you too, will be able to make the life-changing move to self-employment and business ownership.

Constantine Kapothanasis

CHAPTER 1
INTRODUCTION

Figuring it out, defining, and redefining.

Before I begin writing about my business, the businesses I am building, and the startups that I am pursuing there needs to be context on where I come from, and how I got to where I am right now.

My family comes from Kalamata Greece, which is in the heart of the Peloponnese, a peninsula in Southern Greece, and it's located at the juncture of the Ionian Sea and Mediterranean Sea. Being Greek has had an immense impact on me as a human and how I live my life. I have a deep love of my heritage, as it has shaped who I am.

My family settled in Portland, Maine, which is where I was born and raised through high school. I attended Cheverus College Preparatory School of Maine, a Jesuit school known for its academic and athletic excellence. Going into high school and up until that point I had always been known as "that baseball guy." I completely punted school. I had absolutely no interest in school. Although, thanks to my Mom school always had an interest in me. I didn't struggle with school, only because I didn't allow it.

Costa playing baseball for Cheverus High School, pitching Hadlock

My parents instilled a self-confidence in me that probably backfired in a way they would have never expected. From early on, I knew baseball would get me into college, regardless of my grades. There was no subject matter that piqued my interest, besides history which is so typically Greek. There were no business classes that I knew of, and I had always felt that there was no way to really teach business. My Papou had been self-employed his entire life, and my Dad had never worked for anyone else his entire life, and he barely graduated from Portland High School. It was almost a "Well, I guess I will just go that route if baseball doesn't work out" attitude that drove me for the longest time.

Senior year came, I had only applied to one school, and immediately I got in. That was Endicott College. Other schools, I had not applied to but I had been admitted to, were Franklin Pierce University in New Hampshire, Bryant College, Mount St. Mary's University in Maryland, Seton Hill College, St. Joseph's of Maine, and St. Anselm's College of New Hampshire.

Franklin Pierce was a Division II school that was a top five program in the nation that would absolutely beat more than half of the 300 plus Division I baseball programs in America. (Bryant proved this by leaving the same conference as Franklin Pierce, despite being inferior to them, jumping to Division I, and running rough shot on the Northeast Conference.) In the fall, I signed a National Letter of Intent to go to Franklin Pierce as a position player, which is a position other than pitcher.

Thinking about my future and not having used my five official visits that the NCAA allows, I decided my best chance of playing professional baseball was via pitching and by getting the most scout exposure possible. Which is when I reneged on my NLI and went back out into the pool of recruiting. Mount St. Mary's is a small Division I school in Maryland — and partly in an effort to escape the long shadow of my last name in Maine — I decided to sign in the late signing period with Mount St. Mary's University as a pitcher.

Costa and Cait at Mount St. Mary's

For four years, I lived, breathed, ate, and slept baseball, spending every waking moment and thought on how I would throw a baseball sixty feet six inches harder and sharper. This trait is one that has served me well, way after baseball ended. Senior year came and there was only one Major League Baseball scout in contact with me. I was with my then girlfriend, now wife Cait, at a Nationals game when the 50th pick of the 50th round of the MLB draft came and went without my name being called.

Plenty of players sign-in free agency after the draft, and I clung to that hope, and in the meantime, a professional team in an independent league contacted me about signing a contract to play for peanuts.

I'll let Wikipedia explain Independent Baseball: An independent baseball league is a professional baseball organization located in the United States and Canada that is not operated in conjunction with either a Major League Baseball Team or an affiliated Minor League team. Being independent allows teams to be located close to major-league teams without their consent. Such leagues have been around for many years and were once known as "outlaw leagues" due to their position outside the rules of affiliated minor league baseball. (Wikipedia.com; 2016)

I drove to Macon, Georgia, to pitch my first game as a professional baseball player. I was getting paid $300 dollars a week. Although $300 dollars goes a long way in Macon, G.A., when I moved back to Maryland and had some real responsibilities I realized just how little this was.

I then proceeded to sign with a new team in Pensacola, Florida. The team was a little more established and had more MLB affiliated players. I drove from Macon to Pensacola and my contract was terminated after a week and I was out of baseball again, quicker than you can strike out in a game. My quasi-agent, a Maryland lawyer who was helping me pro-bono in the form of making some phone calls, landed me a contract with an independent team in Chicago. At this point I had driven from Macon, Georgia, to Pensacola, Florida, back to Thurmont, Maryland where I was staying while trying to sign on somewhere. It was a truly exhausting time in my life, but it was a passion and you cannot ignore your passion.

Costa pitching for Macon, Georgia first Pro Team

I drove to Detroit, Michigan to meet up with my new team. I got to Detroit by renting a yellow Chevy Cavalier, using my first credit card that I got from the Bank of America. Which is a significant fact because this credit card becomes an important part of my story later. Upon arriving in Detroit, I met my new team and proceeded to sign the new contract. Within a week after signing, I was immediately released again, only this time I didn't stay on the team long enough to even make it to the stadium, or even get a uniform. At this point I was frustrated, I was putting up good numbers, throwing low nineties, and pitching in front of the right people. Why then was I not getting a shot? Later in the season I got a call to return to Macon, Georgia to play out the final quarter of the season, even though the league had announced it was folding after that season concluded. I headed back to Macon, Georgia to play.

While in Macon, I received a phone call asking if I was interested in representing Greece for their National Team. The Olympic baseball team for Greece was founded for the 2004 Athens games because the hosting country is represented in every sport.

I thought *this was my last shot*. The National Team was funded by Peter Angelos, the Billionaire Baltimore Orioles owner. He had let the team hold tryouts at Camden Yards to put together a team of high-level baseball players for the 2004 Olympics. I was sixteen at the time and not nearly good enough to play for that team, which was filled with mostly Major League baseball players, including Nick Markakis.

Costa playing for the Greek National Team Hellas, which stands for Hellanic Republic

The team in 2010, still had players on the roster who played at the MLB level, but for the most part it was Minor League experienced baseball players. I was one of a few players whose highest experience was either Division I baseball or Independent baseball. I pitched well for them, keeping my velocity in the low nineties and even picking up a win against Sweden on the first night of the European Baseball Championship. I remember going back to the hotel thinking *Man, I can say I beat Sweden now. The country of Sweden, I beat them!*

Photo on the Right: Costa playing for the Greek National Team Hellas, which stands for Hellanic Republic

Costa with Erik Pappas MLB Player 4 years Greek National Team

True to the word of a few of the guys on the team, who had contacts in MLB scouting, they vowed they could get me a look from some scouts. I pitched for the Tigers, and then for the Orioles but sadly neither signed me. Done I thought. Done. Done with baseball, or so I thought. What now?, I asked myself.

My girlfriend Cait was extremely supportive, but she's also a realist. She is an accountant by trade. Probably the most rational type of person there is. 2010 was a tough economic year and I was struggling to find work in Maryland. Even the $300 dollars a week in Georgia is more than $0 dollars a week in Cait's parent's basement. I applied to jobs within the field of the degree I received from graduating from Mount St. Mary's, which was Political Science. It was an awful quandary, given the normal transition for Political Science majors is either directly from school to Law School, or directly from school to an unpaid internship with a Non-Profit or Political Organization. I couldn't afford to do an unpaid internship but I had no experience to qualify for a paid position, especially at a time when the economy was so bad. At that point in time, the economy was so poor, you had barred attorneys applying for legislative aide positions.

I took the classes I.S.S.A. offers to become a certified personal trainer. I was still in the best shape of my life and it's a job that

Costa & Cait after Graduation

offers a lot of freedom. This was my first taste of being an entrepreneur, and I didn't even know it. I finished the I.S.S.A. classes which cost me a total of $350 dollars, and it ended up being a fantastic R.O.I., return on investment, because I got a job at the Gold's Gym in Rockville Maryland on Randolph Road as a one hundred percent commission based Personal Trainer. I firmly believe everyone should experience being one hundred percent commission based at some point in their career. It certainly builds character and exposes you completely. I had two forces tugging at me during this time, one inside me that was killing me because I had a boss and was forced to work for someone else, and the other from a more narcissistic place that was telling me this work is beneath me.

This motivated and inspired me to start taking Paralegal classes at George Mason University, while personal training at night. I wanted to pursue a career in Law. I thought Law was the natural progression for my career, as that's what my colleagues from the political science realm were gravitating towards.

At that same point in time a huge event happened in my life. Cait and I decided to move-in together into an apartment in Columbia, Maryland, which is situated in Howard County in Maryland, the second richest county in the entire United States. All of a sudden, my decisions affected more than just myself. I could feel my Mother's feelings by extension. I needed to find what society considered a "real job," and I needed to find it fast. Especially with the added stress of our new place and the county we lived in.

I applied for everything and anything out there. I was continuously rejected by Lowes, Home Depot, Toys 'R Us, Target, and L.L. Bean, despite modeling for a catalog of theirs back in Maine when I was a kid. I also was rejected by the Gap, Nordstrom, and a slew of other retailers at the Columbia Mall. I even applied to TD Bank even though I had not once thought about finance, banking, accounting, or anything numbers-related in my entire life. Math was literally the subject I was possibly the worst at. The manager of the branch, Stacey Hanson, by some stroke of luck was from Maine. If you know anything about Maine, we look out for each other — in any capacity that we can. I got the job after interviewing in the only suit I owned, the one which Cait had bought me. I finally had a "real job."

I was actually good at the job. My numbers were immediately better than all of my coworkers and even my sales were fantastic. TD Bank puts an emphasis on making sure each of their employees is paid a salary, so as to stress their attempt to remove any kind of underlying conflict of interest when it came to financial products for their customers. Had I worked at any of the larger banks in the area during my first year, I would have easily been a six-figure earner in what is considered "the real world."

I finally finished my classes at George Mason University and immediately started looking for work in the field of Law. Soon thereafter, I landed a job with Morris Hardwick Schneider LLC., a

Foreclosure Law Firm, in Rosedale, Maryland. The law firm represented Bank of America and Citigroup and this was during the peak of the U.S. Foreclosure Crisis. Due to the crisis, there was certainly no shortage of work. I was put on a Florida Final Judgment Team designated to get the necessary paperwork in order to send a house into foreclosure.

There are three types of states when it comes to a foreclosure. The three types are Non-Judicial, Semi-Judicial, and Full Judicial. Florida was a full judicial state. What this means is, every piece of foreclosure paperwork needs to be completed and filed with the court before a law firm or bank can foreclose on a property — and this is one major reason why Florida has so many squatters. Semi-judicial means only certain pieces of paperwork need to be filed before they can begin to move forward with the foreclosure, and non-judicial means that the bank can throw a lock on the door before sending anything over to the courts.

Overall, it was a toxic work environment, the poor business structure and lack of organization constantly made me feel like I was in the movie Office Space, trying to do the bare minimum to avoid getting yelled at by eight different bosses. This was certainly no way to live life.

I began the process of trying to create a situation where I was finally able to become self-sufficient. I am a firm believer in the rugged individualism that America used to promote, and can still produce. Rugged individualism is the belief that all individuals can work hard and succeed on their own with little to no government help. I was inspired to file the paperwork for my first LLC during the time I was working for Morris Hardwick Schneider. I was guilty of often working on non-work-related tasks during company time. As time passed, I sensed I was very close to being fired by Morris Hardwick Schneider so I decided to preempt their decision, put in my two weeks notice, and move on.

I turned to Craigslist to find my next job. I wanted to search for a job with practicality. I needed to earn an income to support myself and Cait, because it wasn't about just me anymore. I reached out to Doug John, the owner of Generation Pet which is a pet food distribution company based in Elkridge, Maryland. After speaking with Doug I decided to accept his offer of employment and join his team. He promised after our talks to teach me about the business and relay how he got his start. Doug was the epitome of everything I wanted to be.

Before owning his business, he previously worked in sales for Sysco Corporation, earning a six-figure income, before later turning to his parent's garage to sell one brand of dog food out of a Cargo Van. Fast forward to 2012, his inventory grew and was in the millions. Although I don't know his exact revenues at that point in time, he had fifteen plus employees, as well as a fleet of Mercedes Sprinter Vans worth excesses of hundreds of thousands of dollars. I proceeded to work for Doug longer than I had ever worked for any company before — one year and one month. After a year and a month, I left Generation Pet to go work for the Department of Homeland Security, but that story isn't even worth getting into. Although, I will mention that I almost got fired from the federal government as well.

I strongly desired to have work that I could take home and be proud of. I was struggling to define myself, or even just figure out who I was, and exactly who I wanted to become. When I met my wife's colleagues I was always "the guy who just played baseball" or "the baseball player" which in reality I wasn't, I was more than just that. I constantly struggled with this continuous perception exceedingly for years. I couldn't break free of this paradigm and because of its perpetual effects I continuously felt like a fraud.

Out of practicality and necessity, with my tail between my legs I went back to TD Bank. This time, armed with an M.B.A. that I received from California Coast University, an inexpensive for profit one hundred percent online University. I was in a new role, one that had what I considered some prestige. I had to take financial exams to qualify for the job and I got to stay in hotels for the training, but I was finally enjoying the job. TD Bank saw potential in me and steered me into a partnership they had with New England College, a small school in New Hampshire, which had a business school in Boston. TD Bank footed the bill for me to get my Master of Science in Finance. In addition, in coming full circle, New England College was the very first school to recruit me for baseball when I was only a sophomore in high school.

I dove into the markets and eagerly invested my time in learning everything I could about finance. I started trading my own money quite a bit and being able to be exposed to it at work was a real treat. Everything was churning on autopilot but baseball was still tugging at me in the back of my mind. At least I thought it was baseball.

I founded the Maine Bat Company in 2012. I wanted to pay homage to my home state and also remain involved in baseball, despite not participating in it anymore. This was my first step towards settling my heart and mind where it came to baseball. This entrepreneurial endeavor was pure trial and error at its finest. The first bat I bought and branded was a Rawlings Big Stick which I returned on a lathe machine I bought off eBay. A lathe is a machine used for shaping wood, metal, or other material by means of a rotating drive that turns the piece being worked on against changeable cutting tools. The logo that I used was a rubber stamp I had bought from Michaels the large retail chain.

I was selling my bats to friends at first but I had an epiphany when one of them asked me to put their name on the bat. At the time, having a personalized game bat was extremely expensive. I wanted to carve out a niche and provide inexpensive custom bats and beat out my competitor's pricing. I bought a CNC Router from China and quickly learned how to design CNC images. I started selling a five-dollar margin bat on eBay and I was killing it, making decent revenues on poor profits. How much money I made was irrelevant because I was happy pursuing my passion and the TD Bank job was supporting me financially. I was doing a bat-per-day on terrible margins, but it wasn't work to me because I enjoyed every minute of it. It truly made me happy.

Meanwhile, I felt suffocated by TD Bank. Big corporate bureaucracies don't care about autonomy. You have to "toe the line" regardless of how inefficient the processes are, and you have no say in changing the inefficiencies in the process. At every job I was at, I always felt as though there were things that I could change to make the business better, but at every job that I worked no one was concerned with your opinion or changing and improving the status quo. I was quickly promoted to the Sales Leader of the Mid-Atlantic for TD Bank. I held regular sales team meetings in Delaware and Maryland. In doing so, I received a half-dozen awards at the TD Bank recognition events held quarterly. My name was attracting a substantial amount of attention at very significant levels within the company. I was entrusted and tasked with writing a sales manual designed to help my fellow sales reps better close deals. I was in FedEx in Columbia, Maryland for hours preparing a booklet along with a daylong training event designed to help promote better sales techniques and maximize potential. I felt a freedom at TD Bank that I previously had not felt before, and for a second abandoned all prior thoughts of suffocation. For a fleeting moment, I felt untouchable. Nevertheless, TD Bank brought me back to reality a week later.

    I had e-mailed myself a client list so that I could work from home. I could finally take work home that I could be proud of and I was finally in a position where I could dive headfirst into my work. A lot of people on social media were starting to recognize me as a finance expert and I was often approached for advice and guidance repeatedly. It was important for me to be able to work from home because I wanted to devote myself to my craft. It is a personal trait of mine, and I understand not everyone works the same way.

    I was at work when I received the phone call from TD Bank's Global Security Team, asking if I had sent any personal e-mails from work. Well of course I did, everyone does, the TD Bank e-mails don't allow outgoing e-mails from the @TD.com extension. I was thoroughly confused and I was brought into a meeting room with my assistant manager. It was explained and brought to my attention that the TD Bank team knew about me e-mailing the client list to myself. They allocated that they wanted to have someone physically watch me delete the sent and received e-mails. I had not even opened the e-mail yet, it was still in dark bold text, thus indicating it had not even been opened. The Teller Manager videotaped me deleting it with her phone to show that it was taken care of. The following Monday, halfway through the day, I was promptly fired. It has to be the first time in the history of corporate America where someone was fired for wanting to do more work.

    Armed with a B.A., an M.B.A., and an M.S.F. I eventually found work elsewhere. I worked for State Farm, Merrill Lynch, and finally T. Rowe Price, the fourth largest asset management firm in the country. I always found reasons to leave each job, I either wasn't being true to myself, or I was worried about Cait. Maine Bat Company margins were so low that there was no way I could live off it, but the entire time I was hopping from job to job, my Maine Bat Company was the one bright light in my life that I could count on. There were no Gary Vaynerchuk's or anyone else out there that I knew of that said — "Go for it!" Certainly not my Mom, who is about as Anti-Entrepreneur as it gets. Growing up this always struck me as odd because my Dad has always been completely incapable of working for someone else, and has always refused to.

December 2013 I discovered BizBuySell, the online business marketplace, where people go to sell their businesses. I immediately started researching how to buy a business and using my background in finance, I requested the books from hundreds of businesses to dissect. At the time, I had fantastic credit. My score was damn near close to 800. I proceeded to take out seven credit cards. I then established and set up fake PayPal invoices and essentially sent myself $15,000 dollars. Armed with the $15,000 dollars and my background in finance, I started writing up proposals for business purchases based on seller financing and opportunities hidden within their company's balance sheets.

I will avoid going into further detail here, as I will inevitably explain this later on, but I immediately purchased an existing quick lube in Harrisburg, P.A. With revenues in free fall and horrible management of business operations, I took advantage of a situation and I was able to secure my very own business that in turn had good cash flow.

Later on, I was promoted at T. Rowe Price and moved into a 12P.M. to 9P.M. shift to service our West Coast investors. Working this shift allowed me the time I needed to run the shop from 5A.M. until 10A.M. every day Monday through Friday and both Saturday and Sundays. The new outside business activity created tension with the goliath and dinosaur T. Rowe Price. T. Rowe was and still is stuck living in 1995 and hasn't updated their policies or business strategy to reflect 2016. This is the major reason why so many firms, such as Vanguard, are passing them by despite their massive head start in the game. If businesses don't evolve and change with the times, they eventually decline, become obsolete, or die off over time.

I finally made the jump! It finally happened. I took a leap of faith and left T. Rowe and started running Quick Change Oil full-time. Well, it was more of a push. I was also fired from T. Rowe for what they considered a conflict in the disclosure of "outside business activity." The whole situation was handled poorly which was upsetting because T. Rowe was a fantastic culture. It was possibly the most liberating feeling in the entire world. I don't want you to think I was a miserable person to live with, but if you ask my wife Cait the move was the most positive impact on my life since I was defined as a baseball player. I'm now a full-time business owner. The work isn't work now because it is my life.

From here on out, I want to write about the processes and what I go through on a daily basis. I want to share the mistakes I made, and

provide insight for anyone else who felt and feels like I do. Now that I am here, I am here to stay, and every breath I take revolves around growing my business which by extension is my legacy. At the end of the day, I found out that this is what I care about the most. I don't try to pretend we don't define people, but I would much rather control the definition and how others define me.

Buying a Business with Little to No Money

I strongly believe that everyone has the ability to own their own business. Although, not everyone can or should own their own business, but everyone has the ability to own their own business. I hope that through this book I can give a little insight into the different businesses I have either created, acquired, or sold, using usually little or sometimes no money at all. This is a feasible goal for anyone with the willpower and determination to do so.

We are living in very unique times. We have an unprecedented amount of first generation business owners with no offspring to turn their businesses over to. This is twice as valuable because we have an unprecedented amount of Millennials who have no desire to own their own business. This combo has cultivated an environment that makes it much easier than ever before for us "entrepreneurs" to step-in and take advantage of existing infrastructures and start making money from day one!

Throughout this book, I will write about and explain different ways to acquire an existing business with little to no money up front. I will provide real world examples to follow-up every assertion with, as well as step-by-step descriptions to make the process as clear and as easy to understand as possible. My entire life throughout school I was a C and D student. Therefore, that shows that there is no real trick to doing this, moreso just the hustle, hard work, desire, and want, to achieve the things and goals that you truly want to accomplish in life.

Message from The Author:

I strongly believe deep down to our core, everyone wants to achieve self-sufficiency. The rugged individualist mindset is steeped deep within the roots of our culture and is highly embedded into the American society. People risk their lives daily to get to this country so that they can undoubtedly have their shot at self-sufficiency, and finally not have to deal with no longer being able to call the shots on their own terms.

More millionaires have been created from business ownership than any other means of economic activity in existence. I am the son of an entrepreneur and by and by the product of a country which cares deeply about supporting small businesses. I have always been business-minded and business-oriented, ever since I was a little boy in the second grade when I first sold my holographic pogs at a markup to the other students at St. Joseph's Middle School. This laid the foundation for and lead to my future business-minded transactions, such as selling my Bulbasaur Pokémon card to Meghan Paul for $20 when I originally bought it for $5 at Don's Card Shop in Portland, Maine. My other future business endeavors would include pen and mechanical pencil repairs in Ms. Murphy's fifth grade class. I was especially proud of this business because it was the first time I utilized drop-off services and invoicing.

I later drifted away from business when sports took a front row seat in my life, which lead me down a path that I wouldn't have otherwise chosen. One degree, no debt, seventeen states, and seven countries later I found myself out of sports. I outlined the tribulation of being defined in a certain way the majority of your life, only to have to be forced to figure out a new way to recharacterize, and redefine yourself as a person in my book *"The Grip of a Baseball."* The process of trying to find myself actually led me to my first legitimate business, which I started with very little money.

Entity Name: MAINE BAT COMPANY Dept ID #: T00360816
Ack#: 1000362004760833

Location:
MAINE BAT COMPANY
6 RUNNING BROOK RD
WESTBROOK, ME 04092

Owner:
CONSTANTINE CHRISTO KAPOTHANASIS
1739 JACKSON ST
BALTIMORE, MD 21230

Maine Bat Company Registered in Maryland's SDAT

I will eventually go deeper into the creation and execution of my Maine Bat Company, as it was a key business I began while fully employed, and made profitable within a very short amount of time.

Important:

This book is intended for those with determination, willing to take the initiative. This book will serve no purpose to those who sit and wait for everything to be handed to them their entire life. The work involved requires late nights, many continuous and repetitive tweets, continuous posts on Facebook, as well as on Instagram, and other forms of social media. Social Media Networking requires lots of attention and dedication to continuously posting pictures, as well as posts that at first, fall upon deaf ears. With only the voice in the back of your head that drives you telling you this is the way I should live my life. For some this will be easy, for others this will be difficult. I have been fired more times than I can count, or nearly fired from every single job I have held after attending the University. It made sense to me, down to every last fiber in my body that I should be a successful business person.

Too often at work I found problems with the way things were done, and a combination of pragmatism and narcissism made me believe that I had all the solutions. I continuously pushed the envelope at times, even at the large corporations that I worked at which had protocol steeped in two hundred plus page PDFs called the "Employee Handbook." At times, it was problematic, while at other times I actually created tangible new value for the business. As well as new protocols being created around my initiative.

The security in a W2 job is real, I would never deny that. Some people don't have the stomach to push the chips all in on themselves, and some people don't have the rationale to self-audit, as well as know when not to be pushing the chips all in on themselves. Whatever your situation is, it is extremely important to recognize what is the most pragmatic way to go about achieving your goals. For some, it is turning 7P.M. to 3A.M. into their business building time, and for others it is quitting their job to dive headfirst into their new endeavor. Either way, I want to help and that is what this book is all about. I hope it provides immeasurable value to you.

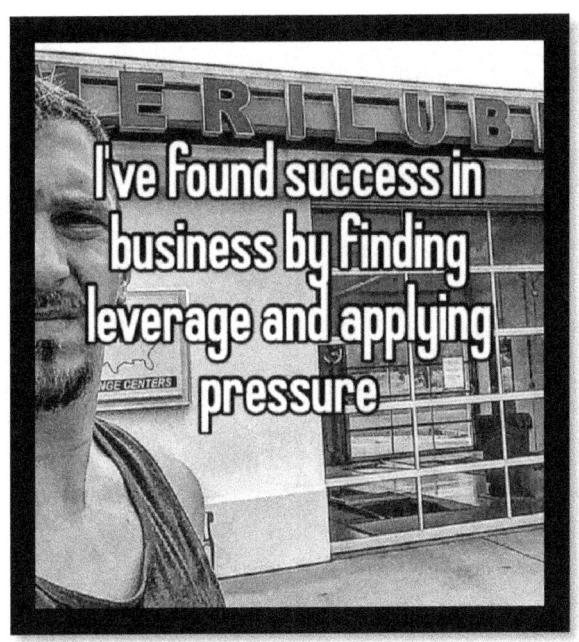

CHAPTER 2
Let's Get Started

Building a business and buying a business are two completely separate things. Depending on what you're looking to get out of the business, one might make more sense than the other. The emphasis of this book is buying an existing business with little to no money. That is where I will spend the majority of my time writing tips, tricks, and advice.

Pre-internet the number one source and really only source for finding an existing business for sale was the Wall Street Journal. The Wall Street Journal to some extent remains a fine source for finding a business for sale, but with the advent of the internet it has become less practical.

Your first stop when looking for an existing business for sale is BizBuySell.com. Bizbuysell.com outshines any other online marketplace for existing businesses for sale. Bizbuysell.com is actually run by staff at the Wall Street Journal, so it was created with some of the smartest business-minded professionals out there. Other resources for finding existing businesses are as follows:

- *BusinessBroker.net*
- *Craigslist.com*
- *eBay.com*

I implore you to tread carefully when dealing with Craigslist or eBay when trying to purchase an existing business. The most glaring reason I can share with you is because typically when a business is listed on eBay or Craigslist it is usually because the owner of the business is struggling. Exceedingly so, to the point where they cannot afford a broker to list and represent the business on the more reputable channels. The flipside to this is that it can create opportunity for those who know exactly what to look for. Sometimes a business owner gets themselves into a situation where they are way over their heads and they need to unload out of their situation as quickly as possible. This can be very opportunistic for those of us who can capitalize on someone else's misfortune. This is partly how I was able to purchase a Vape Shop at a fraction of the cost of their inventory. However, I will get into that later in the book.

Ninety-nine to one hundred percent of the time you will be participating in what is called an asset purchase agreement. Your business entity whether it is you as an individual acting in the capacity of a sole proprietor or whether you're organized as an L.L.C. or incorporated as an S Corp or C Corp, will be purchasing both the tangible and intangible assets of the prior business owner. Tangible business assets would be furniture, fixtures, and inventory. The intangible business assets may be customer lists, reputation, as well as client/vendor relationships. Valuing tangible business assets is incredibly easy while placing a value on the intangibles can be very tricky and can be a sore spot of contention for a business owner who may be selling their business due to a lack in productivity. The business entity will be the owner of the business assets in an asset purchase agreement and makes for a very simple straight forward transaction.

Business Structure

Regardless of what type of transaction you enter into when buying a business, having a business entity is vital. The most common business entities are sole proprietors, limited liability partnerships, and companies, and corporations. Each serve their own purpose.

I own several businesses and I take on a holding corporation structure, that owns all of the subsequent businesses I own and run. The Kapothanasis Group Inc. is a Maryland non-stock corporation that is the sole owner of every business I operate. There are drawbacks to this structure as well, but I have decided that this was the way I wanted my business to be structured. I would advise against sole proprietorships nearly one hundred percent of the time. The sole proprietorship is definitely an unincorporated business along with one owner that pays personal tax on profits in the business. With small government regulation, they are the easiest business to setup or take aside, making them well-liked among individual personnel contractors or business people. Many sole proprietors conduct business under their personal names because developing a separate business or even trade name is not necessary. Sole proprietorship is also called "proprietorship".

L.L.C. Advantages

L.L.C.s protect members, from being held personally to blame for the actions from that L.L.C. This limited legal duty typically protects you inside personal risks involved if your primary lawsuit were to arise concerning your company — safeguarding your own assets. A couple additional great things about an L.L.C. consist of:

- Flexibility in administration: Corporations possess set management framework that place directors to supervise the serious company decisions and the officers enjoy the effect of the day-to-day running in the business. L.L.C.s don't enjoy the same official management composition.

- Pass-through taxation: Along with using pass-through taxation, taxes aren't paid at the company level. If you choose to become an LLC, income and loss are going to be reported on your personal tax return. In case that any taxes have been due, they will be paid relating to the personal level.

Corporation Characteristics

When evaluating categories of corporations, many business people take into consideration taxation as the most important difference between the various business entities. In a nutshell, an S corp can be a "pass-through" tax organization, such as an LLC. In comparison, C corps are generally taxed as individual people. They are also subject to "double taxation." C corporations pay tax on the net profits at the business level and owners pay taxes on the individual level upon wages received because of the dividends, resulting in double tax.

L.L.C. vs. Corporation: Other Crucial Disparities

We've currently noted taxation and management as two variances between restricted liability companies (L.L.C.s) and corporations, but you will discover other key variations truly worth highlighting, such as:

- Company losses: The actual "S corp benefit, " allows internet marketers to use company losses — which include those incurred throughout that startup phase — relating to the personal tax results since deductions.

- Self-employment taxations: An S corp will offer savings on self-employment or simply Social Security/Medicare taxations, and it enables managers to counteract non-business income with losses in the flooring business — in contrast for a C corp the IRS completely separates company taxes.

- Ownership limitations: Neither the actual LLC nor that of C corporation possess restrictions on the quality of owners the business can have or who can be an owner. S companies, nevertheless, have numerous restrictions. S corporations can have no greater than a hundred owners, and owners are not "non-resident aliens." Additionally, S corporations cannot end up owned by LLCs, additional S corporations, or simply non-qualified trusts.

- Returns together combined with venture capitalists: C corps are frequently the preferred incorporation selection of developing businesses. Owners can hold types of stock interests, including preferred and common stock, which permit different levels with dividends. This is one reason purpose venture capitalists select C corporations right after they offer funding to a few businesses. Investors are fascinated by the prospect associated using dividends, often higher dividends, in the event the corporation makes the gain.

- Earnings: S corps can continue and accumulate income, within fair limits, through up to twelve months to a year or more.

N.D.A.s and Business Brokers are the Bane of My Existence

If you ever attempt to buy an existing business or sell an existing business you will inevitably deal with an N.D.A. and a Business Broker. An N.D.A. is a Non-Disclosure Agreement which is a legal binding contract between at least two parties that outlines confidential material, knowledge, or information that the parties wish to share with one another for certain purposes, but wish to restrict access to or by third parties. In signing the agreement, the two or more parties agree not to disclose confidential information covered by the agreement.

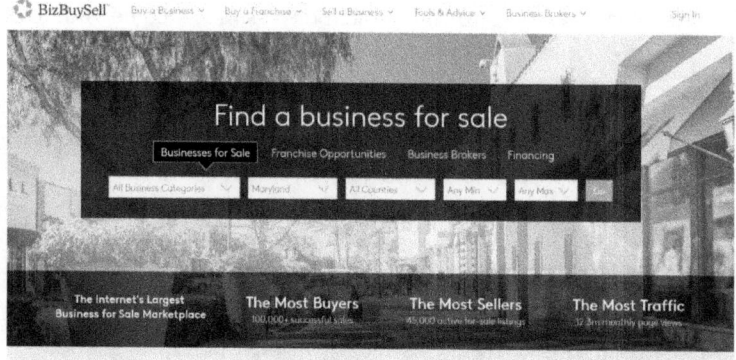

Before I bought Quick Change on BizBuySell I became intimately familiar with both due to the nature of requesting to see the books for each business. Brokers represent the sellers and it is in their best interest to sell the business for as highest possible amount, they are also a barrier to seller financing and other means of buying a business with little or no money because it hurts their bottom line.

Business Brokers

I am not a confrontational person and I am not a mean person by any means — but in my experience, most business brokers are idiots. It's almost as if they couldn't pass the realtor's test so they became business brokers instead. Don't even get me started on realtors now. Business Brokers who are ALSO realtors are a double whammy and I stay away from doing any business or offers with their kind, unless it's a business I'm really intrigued by. Most of the time, the dual brokers are better at one than the other, they are just adding it to the bottom line of their resume.

Brokers never have the business owner's best interest at heart and they are typically over-emotional about the process. Most business brokers have no idea how to appropriately value a business or which evaluations to use accordingly in which situations. Typically, if they are a part of a firm then they have a calculator that they plug in the numbers to and "Poof!— this is how much the business is worth." In my opinion that is a "garbage way" to evaluate and value a business.

Let me preface the following with pointing out that what N.D.A.s do serves an objective. An N.D.A. is some sort of Non-Disclosure Agreement. It is usually referred to as some sort of confidentiality agreement. Be very wary of anyone who will allow you to look at their catalogs without first signing a formal N.D.A. The N.D.A. can be a legal contract between at the least two parties outlining the confidential material, knowledge, or information that the parties wish to share with one another for selling and buying purposes. An N.D.A. restricts access to third parties and is a mutual agreement that neither party will disclose the confidential information shared between both parties.

- When a broker requires me to sign their N.D.A., they're basically declaring in writing, that people don't trust me. It's your right to believe that, but in my own personal opinion it is one way of getting off on the wrong foot especially if you're about to ask me for a favor.
- I have to pay a lawyer to review a document without having any idea why I'm making that investment. No, I won't "just sign it" without having a lawyer look it over, because it's a legally binding document whether a lawyer reads it or not

- If your primary idea is that good, it's very doubtful that it's rare. I hate to be the one to point the idea out, but protecting your idea typically is a fool's errand — good execution is rare to find, but good ideas are abundant.

- I could possibly get screwed through no fault of mine, as a result of some random person walking by me who so much as blurts out that exact same idea that you've had. Exposure to the risk of a lawsuit even if I haven't done anything wrong sucks.

- If I couldn't be trusted with all of your idea, you'd already know about this. There are people who don't enjoy me, or who are frustrated by me, but if I'd broken somebody's trust in regards to their work, I guarantee it'd be the very first thing you'd find when you Yahooed my name.

- The biggest value I can probably offer you is that I would talk about what you're taking care of. If I honor your N.D.A., and I meet a superb investor, or a potential employee, or a valuable partner for a new venture, then I wouldn't be ready to tell them about it.

Most other folks are too nice to really mention it, but since I'm often a bottom line business guy, I'll just say my main point outright: In my opinion asking for you to definitively sign an N.D.A. often causes you to look like an amateur. Not in every situation, but some times.

Now I've had clients use an N.D.A., which can be smart, and I might even do the exact same and ask contractors doing work for me to do so as well. While most big organizations possess boilerplate N.D.A.s that they will throwdown when doing business with new people for important matters, which is not surprising at all. However, for individual online marketers who just have an idea and bigger dreams, they are often misled into believing that providing an N.D.A. will make them look more professional or "serious." Being very straightforward, I believe most individual amateur online marketers end up misled and convinced into the fact that walking in the door providing a fancy legal document will make them look more professional or "serious," when in fact it makes you look like an amateur.

Genuinely thought, you should only share your opinions with those whom you rely on. If you're all for a situation where disclosing a notion could negatively impact you then you've succeeded in finding it. Most ideas gain positive traction and momentum when more people are better informed, included in every aspect of the idea, and are rooting for the person. If you may well, pattern for circumstances the place. Once you're ready to get started talking about one's approach, then you're encouraging visitors to "disclose" your time and efforts, and therefore shouldn't require a contract whatsoever.

On the off chance that I needed to do one for each business purchase that I took into consideration then I would need to monitor these businesses that I am not allowed to discuss. I could then conceivably open myself accidentally to a claim by putting resources into a business with a similar item or even where someone else company is in the same industry as mine. Presently, I'm in a situation where it could be insinuated that since we met and talked then it could be assumed that I was the one who talked first. Not hard when you're putting resources into speicifc divisions.

This brings me to my next reason, thoughts alone are useless. There are most likely more incredible thoughts out there than there are days in every year to even manage all of them. Executing these thoughts and transforming them into a gainful endeavor where I will see a profit on my cash investment is an entirely different ballgame. It takes determination, administration aptitude, income administration abilities, advertising abilities, the foreknowledge, and discernment. The thought itself is useless without these abilities and they are much more uncommon than thoughts.

I have never known or heard of anyone taking a business visionary's thought. I've known about prime supporters or administration going separate ways and thusly contending, yet never a financial specialist. Financial specialists hope to put resources into organizations but not to take thoughts. We don't have to take thoughts. Thoughts resemble grains of sand on the shoreline. You may have an awesome thought regarding a business yet I prefer not to break your air pocket, nor do other people. I would sooner subsidize a business visionary that can indicate their incredible administration abilities, as well as their wise business astuteness to me in an exhausting business where the business thought is a long way from progressive. I would take that any day over somebody with flawed administration aptitudes and a magnificent thought. I peruse many business thoughts and cutting straight to the chase, most thoughts are essentially not worth taking regardless of the fact that that was my express expectation.

Unless you have the capital and intestinal strength to endure a long fight in court where the prime champs will undoubtedly be the lawful calling, which is frequently the case then an N.D.A. is insane at any rate. Who are you joking? It doesn't make you look proficient or savvy it really does the inverse. It's a variety of the "Huge cap no dairy cattle" disorder I talked about quickly here.

I get every one of the commitments and you get none... and yet, you need my cash?! On the off chance that you take a look at most N.D.A.s you'll see that they possibly offer colossally legitimate liabilities for you as a financial specialist with few to none for the originators. It's terrible conduct to request that I sign an N.D.A. without first requesting to meet with me to talk about your business.

Why might you not need individuals discussing your business? What portion of advertising don't you get? This is likely valid for ninety percent of organizations and the other ten percent should presumably be using licenses not N.D.A.s. In the event that you've never met me and request that I sign an N.D.A. then you're letting me know on your first impression and experience with me that you don't believe me. Do your due diligence on me because I'm going to do mine on you. In the event that I've screwed anybody over beforehand you'll definitely get some answers concerning it but when you don't discover anything then you must choose whether or not to trust me. I'm required to trust you with my well-deserved capital aren't I?

1. On the off chance that somebody is requesting cash, make every one of them sign an N.D.A. It'll ensure and make them marginally more terrified of spilling information.

2. In the event that you find yourself approaching somebody for the cash, don't request that they all together sign an N.D.A. You'll fall off looking like a numbskull or a terrorist.

3. In case you're doing genuine business with an organization, you will undoubtedly sign an N.D.A. If one organization's is greater, then you'll use theirs.

My biggest entrepreneurial inspiration Gary Vaynerchuk despises N.D.A.'s and if you were to try and solicit business from him using an N.D.A., he would immediately trash the letter or e-mail in response. His belief is that ideas are crap and execution is everything. I agree with this to an extent, especially when it comes to the new app driven world we are currently living in, but when purchasing a traditional brick and mortar store then an N.D.A. can serve to protect customer information.

When you request the books for a business you almost always have to sign an N.D.A. N.D.A.s serve a purpose, but ninety percent of the businesses listed really do not need N.D.A.'s, but the broker they were using undoubtedly assured them that they needed it, out of some place where they felt the need to self-justify their existence. I extremely hate business brokers, but that is a different story. I requested the books of every Quick Lube from Maine to Florida, all the way to California, and religiously studied them on my own time. I was quickly able to see what successful quick lubes did versus the unsuccessful ones. I was then able to see who was able to get their margins down, and who was paying way too much overhead for their materials. The most substantial thing I was able to do was get the names of potential vendors and distributors which is one of the most difficult things to do in business. At this point I was ready to put in offers to make potential business purchases, but I needed a perfect storm of events to happen for me to be able find an available business. A business that was both proprietary, as well as had seller financing available, and be within a reasonable distance from where I was currently living.

CHAPTER 3
Let's Get into the Techniques for Buying a Business with Little to No Money

The following strategies can be used either standalone or in tandem to purchase an existing business with either little to no money needed up front.

Owner or Seller Financing

Owner or seller financing is one of the most common ways of purchasing an existing business and typically it is a good sign when an owner if offering seller financing to sell their business. This is how I was able to purchase Quick Change Inc, the Quick Lube I currently own and operate in Harrisburg, Pennsylvania.

Business Name History

Name	Name Type
The Kapothanasis Group Inc	Current Name

Business Entity Details — Officers

Name	The Kapothanasis Group Inc
Entity Number	4360417
Entity Type	Business Corporation
Status	Active
Citizenship	Foreign
Entity Creation Date	06/05/2015
Effective Date	05/20/2015
State Of Inc	MD
Address	2720 Walnut St Harrisburg PA 17103

[Form: Pennsylvania Department of State, Bureau of Corporations and Charitable Organizations — Application for Certificate of Authority, filed June 5, 2015, for The Kapotharasis Group Inc., doing business as Quick Change Oil, incorporated in Maryland.]

Banks currently aren't lending to those trying to purchase a business and to even begin to encourage them to look at your own deal, you better have two or three times the collateral with regards to the potential mortgage amount. Irregardless of whether the business is extremely profitable or not and just because they might take a look at your business loan request doesn't necessarily mean they will approve it. Even non-bank lenders aren't lending for the purchase of the business unless the business comes with a substantial amount of real estate, after which they will only fund it depending on a small loan-to-current-value of this real estate. That leaves two options for most of us wanting to purchase the business of our dreams:

- Friends, as well as family, or what a few call friends, loved ones or even fools. Nevertheless, unless you possess a rich wealthy Uncle, most of your family and friends are also dealing with financing restraints and either won't or cannot help you fund a big purchase like that of purchasing a business.

- Owner funding is when the current owner from the business is prepared to sell it to you on terms, thus meaning these people - not the financial institution - hold onto the actual note.

This is what we should and will discuss right here and now, as this may truly be the only method left to buy a business today. Owner financing may benefit the purchaser, you, in many ways:

- It's easier to be eligible for as you don't need to jump through all of the hoops that banking institutions or lenders can make you jump through, such as income analysis, property value determinations, debt-to-income ratios, individual financial statements, and so on and so forth.

- It tends to offer better terms compared to what most banks will offer you – thus, saving the brand-new owner and the purchaser, each time and money – as well as, substantially less in relation to reporting, ongoing monetary statements and taxes returns. As well as, less covenants.

- More than simply financing, since the present owner still has a stake in the actual business's success, they'll provide invaluable assistance and advice well into the future.

- Plus, if the current business proprietor believes in the commercial and you can encourage them to believe in you, then this will be hands down a smart choice for the proprietor. If they wait without giving an excellent reason, that might be considered a red flag to you as it can also show that the present owner does not have confidence in the long-term viability of the business. Their hesitation proves they believe something is incorrect or in decline.

Let's take a look at an example to exhibit how owner funding really works:

> Let's say you discover a business is available, a business that you know you will possess the necessary passion to operate and work hard at. As well as, grow the business well beyond exactly where it stands currently. The price of the business is $100,000, however, you tried to obtain a bank loan and an S.B.A. loan, as well as a non-bank loan. You have also heard nothing back, however, not even a "NO."

Here's where you approach the present business owner and entice them to sell you the company while carrying the actual note. How your own deal should function:

> You tell the present owner that you'll provide some form of deposit, this is to exhibit good faith in addition to providing a small cash incentive to the present owner. This form of deposit should be close to ten percent but might be less depending on how much you may raise. Raising $10,000 is a lot easier than raising $100,000. In addition, any bank or even a non-bank lender might require you to set up more than ten percent, so ten percent is often a win for the potential buyer! Now, if a person put ten percent lower, that means the present owner would

This is how to approach which to do:

> Believe that you'll pay both a principal and a comparable market rate with interest. Let's say with this particular example, ten percent A.P.R., amortized a lot more than seven years. Choose a term for making the payments but be practical as well in regards to the current owner. However, you certainly will likewise incorporate a balloon payment in three years, allowing the owner a total exit if need be or required.

The longer phrase, seven years, gives you breathing room through producing your affordable repayment. The longer the term, the lower the real payment. The balloon repayment, meaning that even though the loan amortizes a lot more than seven years that the remaining balance after three years will be paid off in full. Which affords the current owner a means of getting out in a brief time period as well. This supplies you a period of three years to determine yourself in the industry. When the period does come, you've got a proven track record which you could easily take to the loan company to finance, which will make your balance go up. In addition, if both of you are happy with how things are heading then you can always refinance the quantity, balloon, with the present owner in the actual three year loved one's birthday date.

Now, in the case that you both agreed, you then obtain the business, what you're working for to get started with. The current owner not only sells the company – nevertheless, provided our example, across the board, earns $22,700 in interest above the main purchase price – interest that you just would have obviously paid to your bank anyway, were you to be previously approved for any loan from the bank or non-bank lender. Therefore, you may as well pay it to the owner.

From the case, your payment would be in close proximity to $1,500 per month – very inexpensive and in the three-year increase date the remaining balance is going to be approximately $60,000 – much easier to get a loan approved for as compared to the original $100,000. Really, you, as the startup business person you are absolutely no worse off. From now on you've bought yourself a long time to show both the selling business owner as well as the banks that you're an actual achievement and a great investment or risk. The other issue:

Why, you may inquire, would a present businessperson wanting to get straight from the company be so willing as to owner finance? Well, two significant reasons:

> The business proprietor, given this economy and the reality that banks are not truly lending, might not be able to sell the business an alternate way.
>
> The business proprietor chooses and prefers the positive aspects additionally because he or she receives not only the principal in that loan, what they wanted inside first place, but may also earn

interest in the financing as one's own interest payments visit them and not the lending company e.g. main providing point.

In happy circumstances, for a business to gain success the business owner should be creative in all areas of the business. Within poor times, such as those of today, if you are to be considered a booming business proprietor you should become twice as creative, especially in regards to financing. If you've virtually no other option or solutions, it never hurts to travel to and meet with the current owner and keep these finances – which you do not have to shed. Just come prepared with a deal that has advantages for both you and the owner because owner financing could just be the greatest and last approach to finance and get a company today.

Assume Lease Purchase

Assume lease purchases are exactly that, you assume the lease and take over the whole business. Although, they are very rare and should immediately throw up a red flag anyway. An assume lease purchase typically comes around when the owner has to get the heck out of dodge. They require extra due diligence because owners can say they are retiring or leaving for whatever reason they think you want to hear, all while not showing what's hiding in the closet. The assume lease purchase is the only true way to take over a business for zero money at all. Every once in a blue moon an assume lease purchase will come around when the circumstances dictate the owner leave the business while it is in good condition and standing. This can be landlord issues, health issues, family health issues, or even possibly a lottery situation, amongst other reasons. If you want to look for assume lease sales, you can browse Craigslist or BizBuySell or any of the other broker websites that have a search function. Take the term "assume lease" and put it in quotations so that the search will only bring up results that have that phrase in its entirety.

Move-In Cost

Getting a new lease typically involves upfront cash in the form of a security deposit and advance rent, which translate to heavier financing requirements to start your business. On the contrary, to make their offer more attractive to tenants, businesses looking to get out of their lease can be lenient and may allow you to move in without as much cash. If you are borrowing to finance your business, less cash upfront can result in savings on interest expense. Instead of handing a large deposit to your lessor, available funds can also be used as additional operating capital.

Turnkey Ready

Many retail and office buildings start out with spaces consisting of little more than a few walls and doors. In such cases, constructing the building interior to meet the needs of your business will require more financing and more interest expense payments over a long period of time. One major advantage of assuming a lease is the savings you can get from getting a space that is already finished and does not require many alterations. Chancing upon a lease from a space with a business similar to the one you intend to operate can be a steal.

Save On Rent

Some business owners who are losing money sometimes find it better to assign their lease rather than face the stiff penalties for breaking their lease contract. In such situations, you can save money on rent, because owners are sometimes willing to settle for a lower rent. For example, if a business owner who is paying $2,000 monthly is forced to close shop but decides to rent his space to another business for a slightly lower rate of $1,600 dollars, he may actually lose less than what it would cost to break the lease early.

Location

The location of your business is a major factor that can spell the difference between success and failure. In cases where you have to choose between a location wherein you have to sign a new lease versus a location wherein you have to assume the lease, the location that will bring in more revenue should always be the basis for your decision. A good location can have the ability to bring in sales that will more than cover the rent of a new lease or make the savings that you'll generate from assuming a lease become immaterial.

Cash Advance

Cash Advance was a method I used in addition to seller financing to buy Quick Change Inc.

Date	Type	Name	Subject	Gross Amount	Fees	Net Amount
2/23/2015	General Payment	▓▓▓▓▓▓		2,500.00 USD	-72.80	2,427.20
2/23/2015	General Payment	▓▓▓▓▓▓		2,500.00 USD	0.00	2,500.00
2/23/2015	General Withdrawal - Bank Account			-2,446.42 USD	0.00	-2,446.42
2/23/2015	Website Payment	Constantine Kapothanasis		300.00 USD	-9.00	291.00
2/23/2015	Website Payment	Constantine Kapothanasis		300.00 USD	-9.00	291.00
2/23/2015	Website Payment	Constantine Kapothanasis		300.00 USD	-9.00	291.00
2/23/2015	Website Payment	Constantine Kapothanasis		300.00 USD	-9.00	291.00
2/23/2015	Website Payment	Constantine Kapothanasis		300.00 USD	-9.00	291.00
2/23/2015	General Withdrawal - Bank Account			-1,455.00 USD	0.00	-1,455.00
2/24/2015	General Withdrawal - Bank Account			-2,500.00 USD	0.00	-2,500.00
2/25/2015	Bank Deposit to PP Account			5.25 USD	0.00	5.25
2/25/2015	Postage Payment	US Postal Service		-5.25 USD	0.00	-5.25
2/25/2015	Bank Deposit to PP Account			5.25 USD	0.00	5.25
2/25/2015	Postage Payment	US Postal Service		-5.25 USD	0.00	-5.25
2/25/2015	Bank Deposit to PP Account			5.25 USD	0.00	5.25
2/25/2015	Postage Payment	US Postal Service		-5.25 USD	0.00	-5.25
Total				98.58 USD	-117.90	-19.22

I used PayPal as a means to subvert traditional cash advance methods, ones that depending on your credit can be as high as thirty percent interest rates. Services such as PayAnywhere and Square have made it possible to send money to your bank account for an interest rate as little as one-point-seventy five percent. Cash advancing is not without its drawbacks of course. It can and will kill your credit if you max out all of your cards. Some will view this as a small price to pay to live life on your own terms. While other people will view this as reckless behavior and would never even consider doing it, those people are typically and forever will be W2 employees.

Promissory Note

Instead of putting money down, offer a promissory note. This is by far the most common way to secure a hundred percent financed business purchase. Sometimes, unusually so, a seller financing agreement covers up to ninety percent of the purchase price and the promissory note can get the ten percent needed to complete the purchase. An example of this would be a $100,000-dollar business amortized over a ten-year period at a lower interest rate of seven percent or eight percent. That leaves $10,000 dollars as the down payment. You could offer up a promissory note at a much higher amount but at a much lower term, possibly with a one-year loan of twelve payments at a ten percent interest rate.

DATE	PAYMENT	PRINCIPAL	INTEREST	TOTAL INTEREST	BALANCE
Mar. 2016	$879.16	$795.83	$83.33	$83.33	$9,204.17
April 2016	$879.16	$802.46	$76.70	$160.03	$8,401.72
May 2016	$879.16	$809.14	$70.01	$230.05	$7,592.57
June 2016	$879.16	$815.89	$63.27	$293.32	$6,776.69
July 2016	$879.16	$822.69	$56.47	$349.79	$5,954.00
Aug. 2016	$879.16	$829.54	$49.62	$399.41	$5,124.46
Sept. 2016	$879.16	$836.46	$42.70	$442.11	$4,288.00
Oct. 2016	$879.16	$843.43	$35.73	$477.85	$3,444.58
Nov. 2016	$879.16	$850.45	$28.70	$506.55	$2,594.12
Dec. 2016	$879.16	$857.54	$21.62	$528.17	$1,736.58
Jan. 2017	$879.16	$864.69	$14.47	$542.64	$871.89
Feb. 2017	$879.16	$871.89	$7.27	$549.91	$0.00

Be prepared to factor in that $879.16 payment into the monthly fixed expenses in the business that you're buying, or be ready to come out of pocket for it.

The good thing about a seller who is willing to accept a promissory note, much like a seller who is willing to accept seller financing, is that it shows they are confident in the business they are leaving behind to be able to make these payments. Otherwise, they would be hounding you to get financing through a bank so they can cash out on day one. Which in doing so to me, is a red flag.

Lease to Purchase or Rent to Purchase

A lease to purchase can work for a business purchase, much like it can when it comes to real estate. From a tax perspective, it can be beneficial to the seller. The good thing about lease options for sellers is they can provide a great strategy for any tough-to-sell home off the sector, defer capital gains taxes, and you also gain a tenant who is highly apt at taking great care of your stuff. The best thing about lease options with regard to buyers is that there are so many. Which is a wonderful way to buy yourself some time to figure out your credit or save a greater expense for a down payment. It is just as equally a great hedge against changeable prices. You lock in your final cost now, so if they increase then you'll be protected. However, it's a solution to buy and not a promise to own, so if prices go down significantly in the term of your lease then you can test to renegotiate your price if it's time to buy.

With some sort of lease option there are a couple of required elements. While the rest, is negotiable between the person, the tenant or the buyer, and the landlord or the seller. The way it works is that the tenant leases the home from the landlord. The lease agreement then creates a certain rental rate for a specific lease term. The agreement also expressly provides the tenant the right, or "option," to obtain the property on or after reaching a certain date at a confident price.

Accounts Receivable Financing

Considering buying your competition? Unless you are going to be in business for a decade, establish a wonderful history of robust profit and earnings, have lots of equity inside your balance sheet, and or possess some sort of seller willing to tote the note for your needs, then you will obviously be seeking a version of creative financing. Inside the following pages, we will assume you currently have a business, you've got good quality, unencumbered accounts receivable in the existing business, and therefore you're seeking to find another company. The reality is that most sellers with businesses want all or maybe a good chunk in the sales price ahead of time. Some sellers may finance slightly portion of that sales price for your needs. Often, sellers prefer to sell their establishments at multiples of book value, earnings, revenues, net profit, or all in the above. The value in the business past that book value in the tangible assets is considered goodwill. The more goodwill, the harder it is to finance by standard means. Nearly every seller in the business thinks their own personal business has even more goodwill than everyone else. This is called people nature. Naturally, you produce a business, put in the different sweat equity along with the long hours to access a point that the business has true worth. Now you prefer to cash out also, you want someone to hide what's dear for your needs. The most well-known items creating goodwill include financial records, the customer list, sector marks and sector names.

Consider you make fish an easy food user that hangs some sort of "KFC" sign in advance in front of his store might attract more corporation than his neighborhood friends who hang a great indicator, "Jack's Deep-fried Chicken". Assuming Jack's chicken is a the colonel's, the difference of their sales as a result of goodwill linked to your trade name, "KFC". KFC franchisees invest a royalty to your colonel for getting some of those clients.

Most likely, a company that people acquire won't have the species of name recognition which KFC often enjoys. Just to make sure, you can't justify coughing up an excessive premium for just any name. The name can have some value, but from equity inside assets you're investing in. Most of the value from that goodwill lies inside customer relationships or inside the assets' ability to develop above-market ROA, return on assets. When purchasing the assets in the company, the accounts or simply the customer list shall be included in that acquisition. The value from this customer list may well only be determined after a while. This is the reason why business valuation is accordingly difficult. There are several variables that affect the worth of the clientele list. Customer efficiency after a get is key. The following are some questions to consider:

1. Are you apt to retain the user and or old sales staff in the old business that had the most crucial relationships with those shoppers? Or are they apt to defect and take their customers with them?
2. Can you demand a non-compete from the old owner and will you get the old sales people to sign one?
3. Isn't it time to pay the aged salespeople a "stay on bonus" to cause them to indicate a non-compete agreement?

4. Will your levels of competition use aggressive tactics and utilize the sale of the firm as a root to get the customers to swap to your competition?
5. Are the shoppers contractually bound to remain using the solutions of yours?

Generally speaking, that buy or sell agreement can have a non-compete provision that the old owner will probably need to sign. However, you cannot control the increased variables. The prudent answer isn't to pay upwards of book value for any assets before closing and to hide goodwill. Especially if any variety of, over time for a royalty or quite possibly monthly installment with revenues generated in the accounts existing before closing. Bear mentally, the seller contains the very reasonable expectation that you're going to work hard to increase the value in the customer list by giving excellent service and pricing. It it best to expect the vendor in order to maintain gross sales in deferred or installments to long term gross income. Some negotiating skills are essential.

If the up-to-date accounts receivable are in the sale, then the seller should present you with credit towards the purchase price for any options he receives which hook up with the pre-closing receivables, or the seller should credit for almost any uncollectible accounts after having a predetermined number of days. This can be carried out through using the escrow as described inside the preceding paragraph or being credited. Let's examine a simple case.

Let's examine a simple case:

- Cash: $5,000
- Balances Receivable: $100,000
- Commodity: $25,000
- Accessories (net of depn.): $100,000
- Equipment (net of depn.): $60,000
- Vehicles (net of depn.): $ 60,000
- Goodwill: $160,000
- Comprehensive Assets: $500,000

Financial Obligations:

- Accounts Payable: $40, 000
- Notes Payable: $160,000
- Comprehensive Liabilities: $200, 000
- World-wide-web Worth (Equity): $300,000
- Perceptible Net Worth: $140,000
- 12-monthly Sales: $1,150,000
- Net Earnings: $100,000

Assume the owner is asking $500,000 for any assets, including that of accounts receivable. That has to be a premium of $160,000, in addition to the tangible book value in the assets. Now there are actually two important doubts to consider. Is this company really worth a premium? If so, then the question is how do people structure payments to reduce your amount of risk?

Here's an example model:

- Cash down payment of verifiable perceptible assets minus the balances receivable = $240,000
- Owner collects that pre-closing accounts receivable above during the thirty to sixty days of next closing = $100,000
- Goodwill paid in forty-eight timely repayments is equal to three-point three percent with monthly revenues, to never exceed $160,000 = $160,000
- Comprehensive Sales Price = $600,000

Is $500,000 usually a good price for a lot of these assets? You then might want to consider other company valuation measures:

- $500,000 is usually:

    <.5% with annual sales

    = 6 circumstances earnings

    =150% with market value with tangible assets

For simplicity's sake, we now have ignored other fund requirements such as the debt and equity that the old company continued its books to help finance these means. Consulting a skilled accountant and attorney are critical at this point in time.

Now, you might consider factoring one's own company's accounts receivable to create the $240,000. Then continue invoice discounting both the company's accounts receivable in conjunction with some traditional accessories financing, i.e. leasing or borrowing, to then fulfill your ongoing work capital requirements. After a while, if you are generally profitable then you should be able to retain enough profit to wean oneself off, factoring you aren't qualifying for a personal line of credit from the bank in the future.

Do not composition the purchase to provide a cash purchase in the pre-closing accounts receivable without worrying about the personal guaranty to the owner, quite possibly one hundred percent collectible. You will still verify one hundred percent in the accounts receivable and you will be subject to many risks if you happen to buy those receivables. These dangers include but are not limited to later-discovered theft, disputes with clients, credits, and returns, as well as other dilutive variables. There are practical legalities concerning how the purchasers are notified on the change in remittance recommendations. Anything short with the one hundred percent collectability in the accounts receivable by way of the buyer within sixty days to three months post-closing should to be credited against the final cost in some trend.

Stock Sale or an Equity Buyout

Another way to purchase a business is a stock sale, or an equity buyout. In the stock sale, the customer purchases that promoting shareholders' stock upright thereby obtaining ownership inside a seller's legal organization. That property and the liabilities acquired within a stock sale are usually akin to that of the means sale. Assets and debts not necessarily desired through the buyer will be distributed or repaid before the sale. Unlike a superb asset sale, stock sales do not require numerous separate conveyances of each individual asset since the title of each asset lies inside the organization.

With stock product gross sales, buyers lose a possibility to gain a walked-up basis inside assets and thus do not get to re-depreciate particular means. The basis from the assets before a sale or guide benefits, sets the depreciation basis for any new owner. Consequently, the lower depreciation expense can result in higher future taxes for any buyer when weighed against an asset purchase. On top of that, buyers may take even more risk by purchasing their stock, including but not limited to all contingent risk that is absolutely unknown or undisclosed. Extended lawsuits, environmental issues, O.S.H.A. infractions, worker issues, and other liabilities end up being the responsibility of the innovative owner. These potential liabilities may be mitigated in the real stock purchase contract through representations, warranties, and indemnifications.

If the business under consideration has a whole lot of copyrights or patents, or should there be significant government or even corporate contracts that happen to be difficult to allocate, then a stock sale is a better option. A stock sale is a significantly better option since the organization, not the dog user, retains ownership. Additionally, if a company would depend on a few large vendors or quite possibly customers, then a stock sale may slow the risk of dropping a lot of these contracts. Sellers often prefer stock sales because the different proceeds are taxed within a lower capital increases charge, and in C corporations the firm level taxes are generally bypassed. Likewise, sellers are occasionally less responsible pertaining to future liabilities, for case product liability statements, agreement claims, worker lawsuits, and pensions, as well as benefit plans. Nevertheless, the purchase agreement within a transaction can shift responsibilities for a seller.

The offer structure of any transaction can have a major effect relating to the future for both the customer and the vendor. Many, many, other elements, such as their structure may well influence your decision. It is extremely critical for both parties to speak with their business intermediaries, legitimate counsels, and accounting professionals early on in the process to fully understand the down sides and reach a decision that can produce the required outcomes.

Sweat Equity

Sweat equity takes the right situation and desire. Typically, a sweat equity transfer takes place when a founder has a loyal employee who is tenured and has helped build the business along the way. The owner may be retiring and have no one to leave the business to so they leave it to the key employee. This does not mean that it is the only situation where sweat equity can work.

Sweat equity can be negotiated. Later on, in the book you will learn how to read a basic P&L, Profit and Loss sheet. Knowing how to do so can create further leverage sometimes. If you offer a business owner who is in the midst of running his business into the ground your sweat equity, then you're very possibly working for free for a year or more! It is also possible to hash out a deal where you gain ownership in the business if you can turn it around. Often times, if you are working a full-time job then your biggest asset is your time. If you have the drive, desire, and the want without the cash then this may be your best way into ownership of a business. This is where good business instincts will take you a long way. If you are able to target areas that can immediately improve then you could be well on your way to owning the business, or at least a portion of it.

With a sweat equity situation, I would advise structuring your deal so that it phases the owner out completely. Do it in the beginning so that later on when you have successfully turned the business around you're not stuck being held hostage with a large buyout looming overhead.

Sweat Equity deals can be easier to come by once you're in the industry, especially for the savvy business owner. If you have negotiated good deals and have gotten your margin down, then it's possible to take those savings and amplify them further with the expansion of your business. An example of this comes from my own business. I own several Quick Lubes now, the case study examples of which are included at the end of this book. Outside of payroll, our largest expense that is supplied is bulk motor oil and oil filters. I can offer a potential acquisition, a sweat equity trade-off, if I come in, use my contacts, and utilize better vendors to change the direction of the business.

I would propose a hurdle schedule that phases out the equity of the owner if certain key financials are met. On the back end, the schedule would include a structured payout so that a buyout negotiation can be avoided completely.

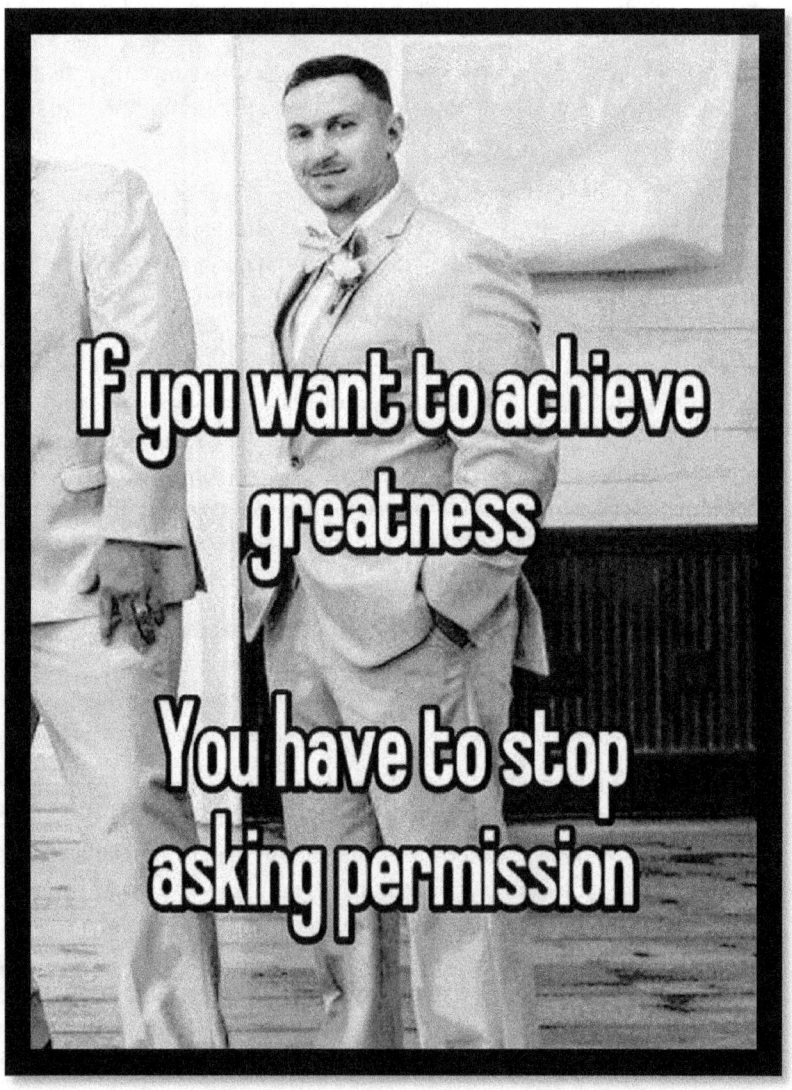

Vendor Financing

Vendor financing is an industry specific and a very uncommon way to purchase an existing business, but much like sweat equity, if the situation presents itself then it can be a valuable tool for purchasing a business with little to no money. Your vendors make more money if you are successful, but if the owner of a business is not doing a good job of running the business then it may be in the vendor's best interest to get someone else in there.

As part of the due diligence portion of buying the business you should always attempt to find out who the vendors are for the business beforehand. If you see a trailing sales trend it may be possible to write up a proposal for the vendor to fund your purchase of the business. This is similar to a seller financed note except the business owner gets his full amount upfront and the payments will go to the vendor thereafter. This is attractive to the vendor because it acts both as a loan with interest and essentially, it's an exclusivity contract where they will be the sole provider of your product for at least the term of the loan.

One quite obvious benefit of "Vendor Finance" is that the transaction can complete, which keeps the vendor happy and you are able to buy a business that you would ordinarily not be able to afford. If the vendor is willing to provide vendor financing this also shows the would-be purchaser that the vendor has a level of confidence in the business. While there are some great advantages, there are also some disadvantages of providing "Vendor finance." One huge disadvantage is that there is a possibility that the business might go bust during the vendor loan period, which would mean that the new owner would be then be unable to pay the loan in full. Another disadvantage is that the vendor does not receive all the money for the business upfront, however at least a sale is made. As fas as the interest charged on a loan is concerned, normally at a higher rate than a bank would pay, the vendor will receive a good return on the loan.

Crowdsourcing

Crowdsourcing has become the millennial weapon of choice.

GoFundMe launched in 2010. GoFundMe is the world's largest social fundraising platform, with over three billion raised so far. With a community of more than twenty-five million donors, GoFundMe is changing the way the world gives. GoFundMe is the only platform I found any success with. I raised several thousands of dollars on GoFundMe to be able to send the Greek National Baseball Team to Holland for a tournament that they were severely lacking the funding for. Although this wasn't a business endeavor, I have seen other people utilize the GoFundMe platform to raise money to launch a product which typically evolves into a business.

Peerbackers consistently recognized among the top crowdfunding websites available. Peerbackers, which was co-founded in 2011 by Andrew Rachmell and Sally Outlaw, operates and focuses on financing internet marketers and innovators. The platform has hosted 1000s of creative, civic, and entrepreneurial projects from around the world. The company recently expanded to incorporate young entrepreneurs from ages thirteen to seventeen through partnerships and student organizations. After seeing such a high industry failing rate in regards to crowdfunding tasks, Peerbackers launched the Crowdfunding Academy to make education and assistance available to those who want to crowdfund.

Indiegogo was originally launched in 2008. Indiegogo pivoted to incorporate funding for literally anything and everything along with becoming known with regard to financing personal and cause-related campaigns. For example, Indiegogo campaigns to keep an eye on for any actual bullied bus, which raised more than $700,000. The following accepts all tasks without assessment because Indiegogo says on its website, "Our platform can end up obtained to anyone, anyplace, to improve cash for anything. " While its success fee of four percent is usually one percent less than the majority of competitor websites , which generally cost five percent, it does charge among the highest fees available -- nine percent -- unless you meet your objective.

RocketHub initially launched with the arts in mind, it later expanded to include science, education, company, and great societal projects. It quickly gained traction inside sciences with its annual SciFund Issue, an online effort to finance science projects. Additionally, it launched a relationship with A&E Networks with which some select projects will likely be chosen to obtain extra support inside a joint initiative.

Indiegogo, RocketHub, and Peerbackers are available to project creators around the world. Kickstarter only allows project creators inside the U. S. and The United States.

MicroVentures brands or calls itself an "investment financial establishment for startups." It conducts research on startups and if approved, assists in raising capital through Angel Investors with its SEC-approved world-wide-web platform. Thus, giving Angel Investors a way to invest small levels of funds to crowdfund the startup.

Angel List, what is referred to as being the *Match.com* in regards to early-stage startups when investors have folded out a great collateral crowdfunding service. It's not for any entrepreneur -- you'll want $100,000 raised now in seed funding and be incorporated in Delaware – however, Angel List contains a convenient system which taps into its strong investor share. It also has the selling point of putting all backers into a single-purpose fund -- an advantage for almost any entrepreneur having to seek forthcoming financing. As venture capitalists, wouldn't or shouldn't manage a multiple of those who prior to this invested.

CircleUp is a distinct equity segment website which has a focus on high-growth, customer product or service, and list companies. CircleUp has joined with Procter & Risk and General Mills to make more value past the loans, thus giving entrepreneurs use of a lot of these brands. There isn't any fee for investments from best friends and family but CircleUp charges a fee as long as you raise capital by having an inventory on its website from brand new investors subscribing with its broker companion WR Hambrecht + Corporation.

Desperate Measures

Liability Financing

Liability financing is a risky move to make, but for the dream of being a self-sufficient entrepreneur it may be one you're willing to make. Liability financing often means assuming the debts of the company you will be purchasing. This can be dangerous in a business that is for sale because it may be tough to recognize whether or not the business is for sale because of these prior debts. I have paired liability financing with other techniques that have been discussed in this book. I would never take on credit card debt, but if the primary vendor has a net thirty agreement with the business then I would offer to take on that debt as a negotiation tactic.

Limited Partner or Silent Partner

I've included limited partner or silent partner in the desperate measures section because it would be considered a desperate measure for me. I hate the need to give up equity to buy a business, but for a lot of people it is the only way to become self-employed. In a case study featured at the end of this book, I entered into a partnership to purchase a Vape Shop in Baltimore.

Broker Loan

A broker loan is rare, as most brokers are worthless but every once in awhile you will come across a broker who has it together. This broker will legitimately be a full-time business broker and not a half time real estate agent and halftime business broker. If the broker understands the P&L and believes in the business, he may offer to finance the deal himself. The broker will get his commission on the front end in the form of a deposit, but then he will receive the interest on the back end from financing the deal. This is not an ideal situation, but it could be a way to purchase a business with little to no money up front. Often times, the perks of privately held notes are no down payment.

Secrets

When I say Secrets, I am mostly talking about little known programs, usually relating to the federal government that can help facilitate the purchase of a business.

"Back Home" Money

That Immigrant Investor Plan, also referred to as "EB-5," has many important sources associated with investment for development projects in the country, thus attracting billions of dollars to your U. S. economy and creating hundreds and hundreds of jobs in America. However, the course is unlike every other mastered by U.S. Citizenship and Immigration Providers, U.S.C.I.S., in the fact that it's the only visa plan whose stated purpose can be to create jobs as well as promote growth. This requirement creates specialized problems and opportunities.

So precisely how exactly does the EB-5 approach work? The EB-5 program has been the only visa program manufactured to allow foreign investors to get permanent residence in the country, via a "green card." It requires the absolute minimum amount investment of $1 zillion dollars and $500,000 when the investment is within a rural or specific high jobless region, where unemployment is one hundred and fifty percent in the national average. The investment must also trigger the creation of at the least ten jobs. You will see 10,000 EB-5 visas available each fiscal twelve months, in a fiscal year.

To be entitled to the EB-5 plan, immigrants can invest directly within a job creating business, or they can commit through local facilities approved by U.S.C.I.S. to encourage economic growth within designated aspects. When the investor's initial software programs is approved, the investor can make an application for conditional residence in North America. Once approved, the conditional residence lasts a couple of years. After many years, the investor can apply to offer the conditions removed and also enjoy the conditional residency created on a permanent basis, but only when the investment has produced the creation of at the least ten jobs due to requirements.

History in the Program

Congress produced the EB-5 Immigrant Buyer Program in 1990 to stimulate the U.S. economy via job creation and capital investment through foreign immigrants. Within its early stages, many years ago, the program had been undersubscribed with only most of the 10,000 available visas used each year. This was within large part a result of a long and complicated application approach, modifications in financial needs, and the idea that denial rates with regard to help, investor petitions were high. In 2005, U.S.C.I.S. created a good Trader and Local Center Unit to boost oversight and inner coordination together, along with releasing new draft recommendations made to accelerate processing and increase the efficiency.

Due to the fact that in 2005 the acceptance prices have improved, the denial price for petitions to take out conditions on long-term residency has fallen from thirty eight percent in 2005 to a low six percent in 2012. Thus, greatly improving chances of success along with the reliability of this program as an automobile for investors to get ahold of residency. Partly due to these reforms and partly in reaction to the tight financial markets produced by the recession, the popularity of the EB-5 program being a vehicle for increasing capital has increased dramatically over the last decade. The quantity of EB-5 visas unveiled to foreign investors increased in the low of sixty-four in 2003 to an upwards of 1,300 in 2008, consistent with some 2010 government-commissioned research just by ICF Worldwide.

The number associated with visas issued to investors in local centers, the finance entities that manage most investment projects while using the program, reached 9,130 in 2014, as reported by the Condition Department. An overall total with 9, 228 visas had ended up issued in FY 2014, which include non-regional center direct-investment tasks.

Precisely what local centers? A regional center can be an economic entity, open publicly and privately, which promotes economic progress, regional productivity, and work creation, together with funds investment. To obtain the state "regional center" name, the entity should submit an indicator to U.S.C.I.S. For approval along with the official "regional center" name, U.S.C.I.S. requires that the proposal show the fact that that center will market economic growth within a geographical region within America.

However, the name of regional centers fails to imply government recommendation, or even eliminate or simply reduce risk. An investor inside a regional center project can benefit from a more expansive idea with job creation, including both "indirect," jobs released collaterally from an EB-5 investment, and "direct" jobs, work created as a consequence of EB-5 invest funds, to be ready to qualify the applicant for that visa. An example of the indirect job is going to be any full-time job in a hotel as a consequence of that hotel being constructed through EB-5 investments which includes a regional center, hired inside the two main years from the investment.

The regional facilities can serve a critical role by vetting traders and investment projects to check high-quality, long-term work creation. Regional centers are multiplying and become the prevalent vehicle in regards to EB-5 expense. As of January 4th, 2016, U.S.C.I.S. offered and authorized approximately 790 local.

What is the legislature doing on EB-5? Regardless of the increased usage from the EB-5 process, this remains a provisional visa approach. Since its beginning, Congress has reauthorized this promotion several times over, the most recent of which was in December 2015. Currently it's set to separate on September 30th, 2016. Congress must act so the program is running following this day.

The EB-5 program is additionally not without debate. A 2015 Federal Government Obligation Office report required that U.S.C.I.S. have better oversight from the program so as to detect and avoid fraud. Especially, the report that incorporated "uncertainties in verifying that the funds invested had been obtained lawfully and that various investment-related strategies were used to defraud people." This offer led a lot of people of Congress— both Democrats and Republicans— to uncover the needed changes to make to this program to enhance oversight and fraud detection.

Presently, there are different bills in your House of Representatives and also for the Senate to reauthorize this promotion with some modifications. One bill in your house would make this program lasting while another within the Senate would reauthorize this promotion for an additional five years.

Employee Funding

Whenever a business is sold to a third party the buyer generally prefers to buy a company's assets instead of its stock, whereas the vendor would rather market the stock. Your decision of asset purchase or stock sale is usually subject to the actual negotiation process and it is an important thing to consider when developing your company's exit strategy. An extremely powerful benefit of integrating an E.S.O.P. inside your business exit strategy is that the E.S.O.P. transaction is always the stock sale, which is generally more favorable from a tax standpoint than the usual traditional asset purchase. When analyzing the cost, it is essential to think about the after-tax proceeds when you compare an E.S.O.P. deal sale to a third-party sale.

In the stock sale, the vendor is generally entitled to long-term capital gain treatment while using the current long-term funds gains rate. The very best capital gains rate happens to be twenty percent plus the extra three-point eight percent Medicare Taxes on Unearned Income above a particular threshold, due to the Health Treatment and Education Reconciliation Act of 2010. The greater common third celebration sale alternative, the actual asset sale, some or all of the sales proceeds are usually taxed at the larger ordinary income price. The top ordinary tax rate is presently thirty-nine-point six percent as well as the additional zero point nine percent F.I.C.A. tax above a particular threshold due to the Health Treatment and Education Getting Reconciliation Act of 2010.

If your sale involves the C Corporation, a stock sale for an E.S.O.P. may provide you with additional tax cost savings. Whereas, a D Corporation asset sale might be subject to double taxation because the company pays taxes on the gain of the sale from the asset and additionally, the seller pays taxes whenever a dividend is consequently paid. There is definitely an alternative E.S.O.P. purchase, the Area 1042 Sale for an E.S.O.P., which allows the vendor to defer or even altogether avoid the taxation of the sale to a good E.S.O.P. The following graph compares the after-tax proceeds of the company sale underneath the three approaches talked about above:

	E.S.O.P. Stock Sale (Section 1042)	E.S.O.P. Stock Sale (Non-Sec 1042)	Third Party Sale
Gross Sale Proceeds	$1,000,000	$1,000,000	$1,000,000
Federal Income Taxes	0	($200,000)	($396,000)
After-Tax Sale Proceeds *	$1,000,000	$800,000	$604,000
Additional After-Tax Proceeds Compared to 2013 Asset Sale (%)	66%	32%	-

* Presently there are additional methods to increase the after-tax proceeds inside a sale to a good E.S.O.P., including extra tax deductions, getting Full Payment from Fair Market Worth, obtaining Additional Value for that Seller via E.S.O.P. Involvement and Synthetic Collateral, and Selling for an E.S.O.P. Obtaining the ten to fifteen percent plus rate associated with return on vendor financed amounts, in the event that any. Including these types of additional after-tax proceeds within the analysis would further boost the additional after-tax proceeds obtainable in a sale for an ESOP.

CHAPTER 4
Mistakes

I am hoping to share some of the mistakes I've made in the past in an effort to help you avoid the pitfalls that I have already encountered. I jumped in head first into business and largely subscribed to the "Fake it, 'til you make it!" mentality. I have run unregistered businesses and I have also incorrectly filed business paperwork. Whatever mistakes I may have made can be your gain. If you know what to avoid ahead of time, it can save you time and ultimately dollars at the end of the day.

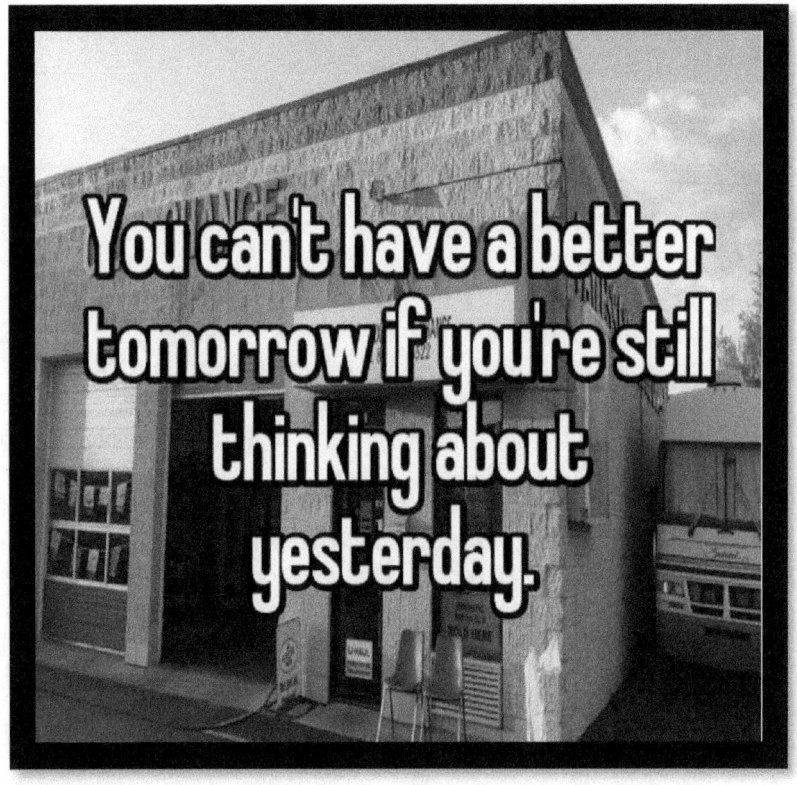

Love

Do not fall in love with the business. I fell in love with Amerilube, a business I eventually got for free. I write about this in the case studies section of the book because I fell in love with Amerilube. Due to the fact that I fell in love with Amerilube, rather than just walking away I had made an offer of $50,000 cash. Which had it been accepted, it would have been $50,000 more than what I eventually acquired the business for. Luckily though, the broker and seller were caught with their hand in the pickle jar. Negotiating is a process of communication between two or more parties to reach an agreement on future behavior, like when you're purchasing a small business, leasing an office, hiring an employee, selling a product, or trying to get a two-year-old to take one more bite of peas. Let's look at the two key words in that definition: process and communication.

Process: Conducting a negotiation is more like running a marathon than a sprint, it takes time and involves multiple steps. By accepting this reality you'll set yourself up to be more patient and therefore, more effective.

Remember, your impatience with the process is the other party's best leverage. Good negotiators practice patience.

Communication: There are many ways to communicate in a negotiation besides speaking: Punctuality, appearance, organization, and attention to detail, for example, are all forms of communication. You could even communicate in absentia with the quality of the documents you produce.

Never underestimate the heightened awareness of every aspect of a negotiation. The slightest nuance, gesture, or facial expression can mean something. Make sure all communications contribute to your negotiating objectives. There are three critical questions to ask yourself before any negotiation:

1. What do I want?

Make sure you have this conversation with yourself. If you don't know what you want, how will you know when to stand firm and when to give something away? If the other party senses you're not focused, they will either disengage or view you as weak prey and take advantage. Either way, you lose.

2. Why should the other party negotiate with me?

If a genie grants you one wish prior to a negotiation, ask what motivates the other party. Armed with that perspective you can get the other information you'll need in due time.

3. What are my options?

The best way to get what you want in any negotiation is if you don't have to do the deal. Having an alternative to what's on the table strengthens your ability to walk away from a deal that isn't moving in your favor. It doesn't have to be perfect-just an alternative. Sometime during the negotiation, your second choice might start looking pretty good. And merely knowing you're in a position to walk away will make you a better negotiator.

Finally, whatever you do, don't fall in love with any deal unless you want to make the other party's day. Love is for lovers, this is business. Remember... Everything's negotiable.

Silence

Don't ever show or overplay your hand. I further outline some strategies for the upcoming section on negotiating deals. Now, you don't have to be Donald Trump to make a great deal but you can shoot yourself in the foot by letting on interest too early, or by not showing enough interest to be considered. If you are new to negotiation, or feel it is an area where you can improve here are the most important things not to say:

1. The word **"between."** It often feels reasonable—and therefore like progress—to throw out a range. With a customer, that may mean saying "I can do this for between $10,000 and $15,000." With a potential hire, you could be tempted to say, "You can start between April 1st and April 15th." However, that word between tends to be tantamount to a concession, and any shrewd negotiator with whom you deal will swiftly zero-in on the cheaper price or the later deadline. In other words, you will find that by saying the word between you will automatically have conceded ground without extracting anything in return.

2. **"I think we're close."** We've all experienced deal fatigue: The moment when you want so badly to complete a deal that you signal to the other side that you are ready to settle on the details and move forward. The problem with arriving at this crossroads, and announcing you're there, is that you have just indicated that you value simply reaching an agreement over getting what you actually want. Whereas, a skilled negotiator on the other side may well use this moment as an opportunity to stall, and thus to negotiate further concessions. Unless you actually face extreme time pressure, you shouldn't be the party to point out that the clock is loudly ticking in the background. Create a situation in which your counterpart is as eager to finalize the negotiation, or better yet, more eager, than you are!

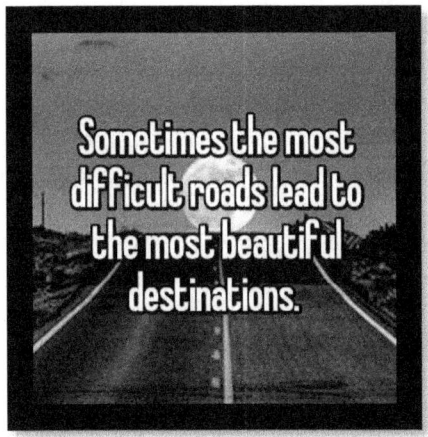

3. **"Why don't you throw out a number?"** There are differing schools of thought on this, and many people believe you should never be the first person in a negotiation to quote a price. Let the other side start the bidding, the thinking goes, and they will be forced to show their hands, which will provide you with an advantage. Although some research has indicated that the result of a negotiation is often closer to what the first mover proposed than to the number the other party had in mind. The first number uttered in a negotiation, so long as it is not ridiculous, has the effect of "anchoring the conversation." One's role in the negotiation is important, too. It can play a determining factor as well. In the book, *Negotiation*, Adam D. Galinsky of Northwestern's Kellogg School of Management and Roderick I. Swaab of INSEAD in France write: "In our studies, we found that the final outcome of a negotiation is affected by whether the buyer or the seller makes the first offer. Specifically, when a seller makes the first offer, the final settlement price tends to be higher than when the buyer makes the first offer."

4. **"I'm the final decision maker."** At the beginning of many negotiations, someone will typically ask, "Who are the key stakeholders on your side, and is everyone needed to make the decision in the room?" For most entrepreneurs, the answer, of course, is yes. Who besides you is ever needed to make a decision? Isn't one of the joys of being an entrepreneur that you get to call the shots? Yet in negotiations, particularly with larger organizations, this can be a trap. You almost always want to establish at the beginning of a negotiation that there is some higher authority with whom you must speak prior to saying yes. In a business owner's case, that mysterious overlord could be a key investor, a partner, or the members of your advisory board. The point is, while you will almost certainly be making the decision yourself, you do not want the opposing negotiators to know that you are the final decision maker. Just in case you get cornered as the conversation develops. Particularly in a high-stakes deal, you will almost certainly benefit from taking an extra twenty-four hours to think through the terms. For once, be "falsely" humble, pretend like you aren't the person who makes all of the decisions.

5. "Fuck you." The savviest negotiators take nothing personally, they are impervious to criticism and impossible to fluster. And because they seem unmoved by the whole situation and unimpressed with the stakes involved, they have a way of unnerving less-experienced counterparts. This can be an effective weapon when used against entrepreneurs, because entrepreneurs tend to take every aspect of their businesses very personally. Entrepreneurs often style themselves as frank, no-nonsense individuals, and they can at times have thin skin. However, whenever you negotiate, always remember that it pays to stay calm. Never show that an absurdly low counter-offer or an annoying stalling tactic has upset you. Use your equanimity to unnerve the person who is negotiating with you. And if he or she becomes angry or peeved, don't take the bait to strike back. Just take heart, you've grabbed the emotional advantage in the situation. Now go close that deal!

Trust

Putting your trust in someone else may not come easy for you, if you are the type of person who puts their trust in themselves first and foremost, or else you wouldn't be reading this book. However, if you are a trusting person, really take the time to thoroughly evaluate everyone you deal with during this period. In order to be a successful negotiator, you are going to have to build a reputation that makes others want to negotiate with you. One of the most important parts of this reputation is going to be just how much the other side of the table trusts you. Yes, you can use all of the negotiation styles, negotiating techniques, and dirty tricks that you want in order to get your way during a negotiation however, this will cause others to not trust you. In doing so, you'll be harming yourself in the future. Just exactly what is this trust thing and how can you earn it?

What Is Trust? We all know what trust is, right? Well, when it comes to negotiating trust can be a very slippery thing indeed. Considering the fact that the reason that you've entered into negotiations with the other side of the table is because you want to be able to reach a deal with them, ultimately trust is the thing that is going to allow both sides to reach a good-faith deal.

One of the most important things that any negotiator must realize is that you never want to enter into a negotiation with someone that you don't trust. This lack of trust means that you really consider the other side of the table potentially to be a thief. No matter what kind of deal you are able to strike with this type of person, you know that you are just going to have a lot of heartaches involved in getting them to do what they have promised you that they would do.

There are some deals, that when we discover them, simply look too good to be true. The bad news is that they generally are. When you find deals like this, it is perfectly natural to start to doubt the other side's ability to deliver. You need to skip deals like this and focus on the ones where doubt and suspicion can be removed from the bargaining table. You need to be able to negotiate without having to fear that the other side won't do or follow through with what they've promised.

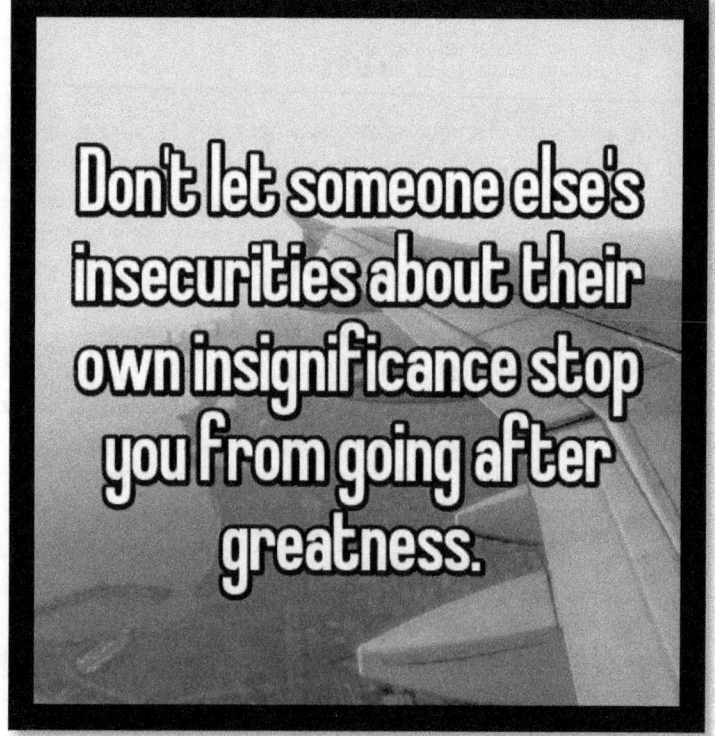

How Do You Create an Atmosphere of Trust?

In order for a negotiation to proceed to a close and a deal, you are going to have to create an atmosphere of trust that both sides can feel during the negotiations. This is where some of the tricky points will start to come up.

One of the most important is that "trust" does not mean that you always have to be agreeing with the other side of the table's demands. In fact, you have permission to do whatever you feel that you have to do during a negotiation in order to gain an upper hand during the negotiations. Note that this does not mean that you can do anything that is either illegal or immoral, but outside of those things, just about anything else goes.

During the negotiations, you should feel free to say things that don't relate to your bottom-line position but which rather are simply positioning statements for your negotiations. Trust has to do not so much with what you say during a negotiation, but rather with what you will finally end up agreeing to do. Being true to your word is what trust in a negotiation is all about.

What Does All Of This Mean For You?

As a negotiator, your goal needs to be to develop a reputation that will make others want to negotiate with you. A key part of such a reputation is to get the other side of the table to trust you. Trust is what is going to make the other side want to do a deal with you in the first place. You need to understand that during a principled negotiation, you may assume many different positions and this won't affect how much the other side trusts. However, it's the final agreements that you reach and your ability to fulfill them in the end that will determine how much trust you have earned.

No, you don't need trust to reach a deal with the other side of the table. You can trick them, promise them the world, and then deliver very little. However, your actions from this negotiation will set the stage for your next negotiation and things will only become more difficult for you if you don't take the time to build a reputation based on trust starting with your next negotiation.

Cash Businesses

Cash businesses tend to have funny-looking book keeping. This tends to go back to trust. Some prime examples of these cash businesses are as follows:

- Barber Shops
- Liquor Stores
- Nail and Hair Salons
- Vending Machine
- Food Truck
- Some Restaurants
- Laundromats
- Bakeries
- And etc.

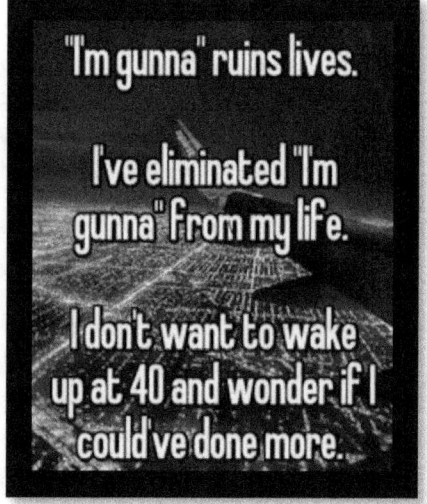

From a buyer's perspective, how can anyone possibly pay for something they cannot prove? Talk about someone being out of their mind that is the definition of insanity. Why would anyone ever buy a business based upon the seller telling them "there is plenty of cash that comes in that I don't report" (wink, wink).

As a business owner, unreported income is not only illegal, it is plain stupid. First, I guarantee in any business, if the owner is stealing money, so too are the employees. Second, instead of taking out cash, reinvest it in the business. The potential growth that can result can be infinitely greater than what the seller "got away with". Third, since businesses are sold at multiples, all revenue and the resulting additional profits will yield a factor of two, three, or four times the amount.

Unfortunately, many business owners get into the habit of taking cash and their lifestyles require it. If that is the case, then at the very least have enough foresight to halt the practice at least a year before you may be planning to sell the company so a buyer can validate the income.

As a buyer, never get fooled into paying for something a seller cannot prove. In any business I have ever purchased when a seller expects me to pay for the cash they cannot prove, I always offer to pay them a multiple of the cash after I have had a chance to measure it for two years after the sale. To this they always respond: "How can I know that what you are telling me will be correct?" and to that I always respond" "That is exactly my point. If you cannot trust my figures how can I trust yours?" I win every time.

If you run a business, then run it properly. Put all of the income on the books. Doing anything else is not only illegal and cheats the government, it cheats yourself from investing more into the business and detracts from the added value you will leave on the table when the time comes to sell.

CHAPTER 5
How to Read a P&L Report

██████ LLC
Profit & Loss
January through December 2013, 2014 2015 with Add-backs

	2015	2014	2013
Ordinary Income/Expense			
Income			
Sales	207,529.38	224,801.67	164,731.42
Total Income	207,529.38	224,801.67	164,731.42
Cost of Goods Sold			
Merchant Account Fees	4,579.47	4,469.20	2,357.00
Parts Purchases	38,014.11	42,652.77	39,262.00
Total COGS	42,593.58	47,121.97	41,619.00
Gross Profit	164,935.80	177,679.70	123,112.42
Expense			
Advertising and Promotion	219.35	192.26	301.00
Auto & Truck Expense		1,505.83	1,128.00
Bank Service Charges	279.99	846.96	156.00
Insurance Expense	6,000.00	6,000.00	6,000.00
Interest Expense	20.00	174.70	
Legal & Professional Fees	900.00	900.00	3,543.00
Loan Payment/Rent to 1756	31,339.00	37,606.80	34,004.00
Meals and Entertainment	28.57	229.13	53.00
Office Supplies	541.60	240.08	371.00
Payroll Expenses	59,616.61	65,381.00	51,711.00
Payroll Taxes and Fees	7,143.78	6,141.00	
Professional Fees	150.00	3,150.00	
Repairs and Maintenance	1,673.74	273.44	
Sales Tax	9,047.18	9,519.18	6,791.42
Taxes/Property Taxes	12,000.00	12,000.00	12,000.00
Telephone Expense	1,830.11	2,436.07	964.00
Utilities	5,675.18	6,493.30	5,060.00
Total Expense	136,465.11	153,089.75	122,082.42
Net Ordinary Income	28,470.69	24,589.95	1,030.00
Add-Backs:			
Loan payments by Elite	31,339.00	37,606.80	34,004.00
Manager Salary	40,000.00	40,000.00	40,000.00
Payroll Taxes - Manager Salary	4,800.00	4,800.00	4,800.00
1 Estimated Loan Payments - New Owner	-18,103.56	-18,103.56	-18,103.56
Net Income Adjusted for Add-backs	86,506.13	88,893.19	61,730.44

1 Estimated payments based on $395,000.00 loan (20% Down) @ 4% for 25 years

Actual P&L of a Quick Lube I am currently pursuing at the time of writing this book (Update 1/20/2017 I have purchased this business in Pittsburgh)

Reading a P&L report gives you leverage. A good amount of business is finding leverage and using it to whatever is most advantageous to you. This is probably why some of the most successful business people are considered cold and calculating because they know exactly how to utilize leverage.

Sales

Revenue, also called the "top line" in the P&L, is the money that you're earning from your sales. If you're some form of non-profit, this would then be profit raised from fundraising. Usually, an organization will have a separate bench that details their sales and brings the total sales number to the P&L. Of course, revenue is a pretty critical number as it is what you should use to cover your expenses. The bigger the decrease in your revenue number, the lower your expenses should be in order to stay successful.

Cost of Goods Sold or C.O.G.s

Cost of Goods Sold, or C.O.G.s, are typically the costs that you incur as soon as you make your products or offer your services. You don't incorporate rent or payroll in these totals, but you would include things that directly contribute to each of your sales. For example, for a bicycle shop, the direct cost of each one sale is what the shop paid to own the bikes from the company. For a bike manufacturer, direct costs would include the money necessary to buy the metal and plastic needed to make each bike. However, when you're a consultant, it's possible you've got very low or even virtually no direct costs. You might have costs with printing reports, photocopying, and office supplies, but not very many other costs. To learn even more about direct costs, read some of our article that explains things in more detail.

Gross Profit

To factor to your gross profit, subtract your direct costs out of your revenue and there you have one's gross margin. Gross margin tells you the amount of money you have leftover to cover your expenses after you've already covered the money necessary for the product or service you will be selling. The Gross Profit percentage represents that number as a percentage—the higher the number the better. When you have an excessive gross margin, that means that it costs you almost no money to deliver your product and you'll have the vast majority of money from every sale left to cover your expenses.

Expenses

Operating expenses cover the different expenses that you incur for your doors to remain open, excluding your direct costs that we talked about earlier. This continually includes your rent, salaries together combined with benefits, marketing expenses, research combined together with development expenses, utilities, and so on and so forth. Don't include interest that you pay for on loans or taxes though.

Net Ordinary Income

Operating income is often called E.B.I.T.D.A., earnings before interest, duty, depreciation, and amortization. This is calculated by subtracting operating expenses out of your gross margin. You started with all your revenue as your "top line" and subtracted things as you journeyed through the process, such as direct costs, operating expenses, or anything else of that matter. What's left over is one's profit, or potentially your loss if you happen to end up spending more compared to what you earned. Some people call this the bottom line.

Negotiating the Cost

Once you have your loans, cash, or even the hopes of a free business, it is then time to find the company that you want to buy. If you are stuck, your accountant can assist you by helping you understand and letting you know how much you'll be able to afford to purchase in the market. Just as soon as you can account for a financial troubles service within operating capital requirements. There are several factors to take notice of.

It's extremely useful to take into consideration who you are generally speaking with. Most sellers are of the mindset that, regardless of the categories of business they set in position for a sale, they will believe it's worth upwards of what it actually is. Particularly, if there's an emotional attachment for this business. If the seller founded that firm or it's been an important part of his or her life, along with impact it has had on the lives of his friends together combined with family, then you the buyer might consequently realize it's trickier to realize a price. Sellers may also have their personal debt to consider, which can possess an important influence on driving inside asking price, advises Chad Simmons, author of the market Valuation Bluebook.

Protect yourself from the inside potential pitfalls from that of the economy. One method to accomplish that, should be tied to the main purchase price so that it will insure future earnings. They are typically called performance-based offers and get outs. The following doesn't only construct some insurance to meet your needs as the buyer should short-term sales have at least one dip, but it also puts the owner on the spot when it comes to putting their money where their own mouth is. If the business is consistently as great as reported by users it can also be that the seller should be able to remain flexible about this principal offer, especially when you're at an impasse inside negotiation.

You can end up conscious with potential complications inside dialogue. Sometimes, the back and forth of negotiating a measure can get complex pertaining to unexpected factors. For example, in the case in March 2007, Brian Douglas was finalizing a deal all-around to get a custom cabinet manufacturer situated in Los Angeles. Douglas said that he wasted many months searching for his great opportunity he could take advantage of and he was considering the potential of the main company -- which had a decent reputation with house contractors, as well as good Earnings. In particular, he paid attention to the Taxes, Depreciation, and Amortization, E.B.I.T.D.A. of the company, and offered $5 million dollars. The rub was that that company's founder, was an accomplished Argentinean craftsman, who had just as of late died. That meant Douglas was negotiating with the founder's widow, who had a highly emotional attachment towards the sector her spouse had produced and built from the ground up, as a result from scratch. After several months, together combined with five trips via airplane for Douglas, the deal dropped separately because he wasn't hoping to pay the selling price with the vendor who didn't want any type of a performance-based generate available. "In final, I thought the value was too risky for just anyone to accept, inch your pet says.

Always construct in conditions so that it will break and prevent an impasse. The very best advice to give on busting a terrific impasse, states Peter Berg using Transworld Business Agents with Florida, would be to produce an offer with at least one letter of intent, L.O.I., that's contingent on the vendor proving that just the thing they say concerning the sector is accurate. In other words, build conditions into your offer to protect yourself if you uncover certain aspects. Building in conditions allows an uncomfortable person to slow down the purchase or better negotiate a price, especially if they uncover aspects that make them want to slow down or bail on terms altogether. Where the business stands, although the scrutiny you will offer it in the homework stage that follows, the price may stay firm. One thing to consider, however, is that on no account should anyone ever pay the vendor any cash before the close of the final deal. If you prefer some type of show of great confidence, you can place a deposit of ten percent of the value inside an escrow account as an alternative.

CHAPTER 6
Conclusions

In conclusion, know your own risk tolerance. If you're anything like I am it is probably very high.

My Favorite Perk of Business Ownership

I can produce new content every single day. That particular fact, is not my favorite perk of business ownership but it's a byproduct of my favorite perk of business ownership. Every day I learn and see something new. Whether it comes from a vendor, a client, a customer, or even the government I learn something new every single day of being self-employed. I used to think when I was working at TD Bank that I had a similar situation, but in retrospect it is not even close. While I had multiple new situations every single day, which is the nature of any retail job, the variations of the situations were finite, the resolution, and outcome were almost always in the hands of someone else.

Being the boss, President, CEO, owner and operator, or whatever title you so see fit to designate yourself as, means the buck stops with you. You own your own decisions. I have a manager at Quick Change who I give a great deal of latitude to as he has been in the industry a hell of a lot longer than I have been. However, when it comes to dealing with out of the ordinary, non-shop operational decision-making then everything passes through me. Which means I need to consider all the variables when making the final decision. Picking and choosing your battles is the name of the game for me. We live in an age of digital transparency and one wrong decision could bring your business down, or at least maim it.

What does this have to do with learning something new every day? The ongoing battles of daily business ownership consist of you asking people for money and people asking you for money. Whether it is battling vendors for the necessary products to run the business or battling invoice holders who are behind on their net thirty. This also includes the battles with the customers who are paying for your service. When is it right to wave the white flag and refund? When do you stand your ground, and tell the person to take a hike? The daily situations that you encounter give you perspective and allow you to learn the little nuances on how to handle bigger situations in your business as well as in life.

Side Note:

The first day I was not employed by someone else it felt like a 10,000-pound Elephant got up from sitting on my chest. I was literally suffocating working for someone else, it affected how I treated other people, and as well how I felt about myself. The reason this isn't my favorite perk of being self-employed is because I recognize that this is not the case for everyone. I feel normal now. I feel more alive and more like myself. I don't view it as a perk, I just feel like I am living the life that I was always intended to live.

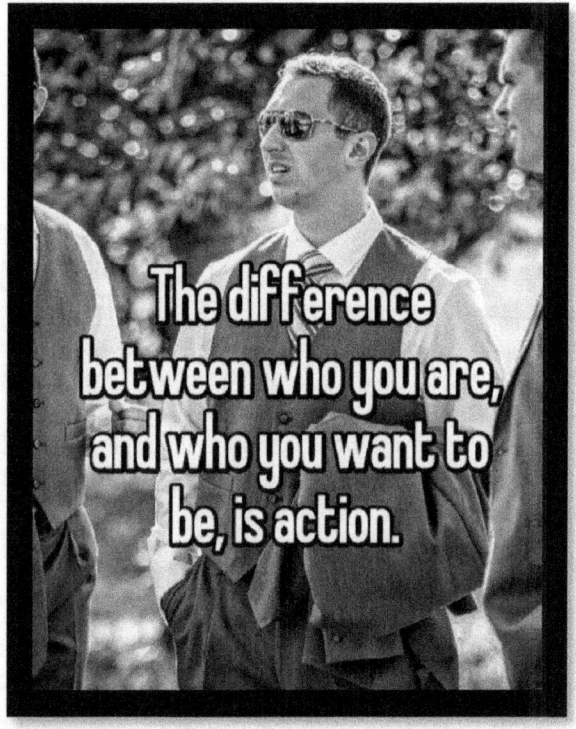

CHAPTER 7
Case Studies

Here are some case studies that show that all of this is possible.

Quick Change 10 Minute Oil Change In Harrisburg, Pennsylvania: Little Money

Quick Change was my first business and the story of how I took over the business is worth telling. Quick Change was listed on BizBuySell for $449,000. It was one of the hundreds of books I requested while in search of a quick lube business to buy. I knew I didn't have $449,000, but it was more research than anything at that point in time. $300,000 represented the real estate while $149,000 represented the business value. I was in no position to purchase the real estate but I was interested in the business. Since the owners of the business were also the owners of the property then that would make them the landlords as well.

I made so many mistakes during this process it is almost embarrassing to write about, but in hindsight I was blinded by my want to own my own business, consequently I missed a lot of red flags. I was still working full-time at T. Rowe Price when I decided to put in an offer on Quick Change. My first offer was $50,000 for the business and blindly accept the lease amount. This was a far cry from the $149,000 the sellers were asking for. I told them that the real estate was off the table but I would move quickly if they would sell me the business by itself. They counter offered at $100,000 and I came right back at $85,000 with 10% down. They quickly accepted these terms, which in hindsight, given the greedy penchant my landlords later on would exhibit made this seem like the deal of the century.

At this point in time I was at my parent's house in Maine because my Grandfather had passed away. I had to move quickly to come up with the $8,500 down payment, along with the security deposit, and the first month's rent. I rushed to sign-on to PayPal and took out all the credit cards that I previously applied for and quickly forwarded myself the funds. After I procured the funds, I scheduled a time to meet up with the owners and sign the asset purchase agreement in downtown Harrisburg. We met up at the agreed upon location, I reviewed the agreement, signed, and it was done. I finally did it, I owned my own business. I was one hundred percent in charge. After signing, I maintained my job at T. Rowe price for a few months longer before the jump to full-time self-employment. Once I was all in, I knew there was no going back.

City Vape in Baltimore, Maryland: Little Money

City Vape was originally Gypsy Vape, a business founded by two buddies who had the ultimate goal to purchase a bar in downtown Baltimore. They didn't have a true passion for vaping but they did have a true passion for margin and during that time vaping, prior to certain regulations recently passed, had fantastic margin. The guys at Gypsy Vape organically grew the business and eventually opened two other locations in succession. Over time, they had to face the fact that one of their bars was failing. After awhile, they realized in order to sustain the failing bar they would have to make a decision and fast. They proceeded to do their own calculations and came to an agreement that if they sold one location they would then have the necessary means and cash flow from the other two to sustain the failing bar.

The negotiating wasn't difficult because it was easy to see they were dying to get out. This type of desperation is prime leverage. This was a classic asset purchase agreement. They walked on their lease and said whatever is left behind is yours. The actual bill of sale for Gypsy Vape was done on a napkin at the bar they opened. The duo originally wanted $49,000 for an outright sale of the entire business. After negotiating, stalling, more negotiating, and more stalling, we finally came to an agreement on a purchase price of $17,500. However, I didn't have $17,500 and I certainly didn't have that for a vape shop, an industry that I had no real interest in.

Eventually, I utilized a fifty-fifty partnership strategy to purchase this new business. Now I had no money at the time, so my value came from my experience owning a business. However, this is typically not a strategy that can be used for a novice business owner, that is unless you have an extremely generous friend. With the capital put up by my business partner we immediately went to work on turning the shop around. I was proud of myself, I officially owned two businesses without coming out of pocket. We decided to change the name to City Vape and I also designed the logo.

Oleum Oils in Westminster, Maryland: No Money Scaling the Unscalable Business

Oil changes are a quasi-utility. Nearly everyone in America drives and car ownership is extremely high, which means that the number of people getting oil changes is also high. The vast majority of oil changes fall into three categories — you either do them yourself, have the car dealership do them for you, or you go to a quick lube, such as Quick Change.

When I first took over Quick Change I was looking into various ways I could grab market share from the dealerships, as well as the D.I.Y.ers. As it stands, an oil change shop is not a scalable business. A shop's demographic is often limited to a specific geographic location, therefore when it comes to advertising, I am not a fan of Facebook Ads because they jump from a ten to a twenty-five-mile radius. I believe a fifteen-mile radius is a good area to cover for a high-quality oil change, as well as target a certain age group. Trying to attract, lure in, and grab the D.I.Y.ers seems to be a losing battle, as these people are typically intimately attached to their vehicle. Whereas, the dealership folks can be an extremely tough grab when they get free oil changes for the purchase of their vehicle for a limited period of time. Therefore, the angle we ultimately take with grabbing the dealership folks is we offer no appointments necessary and we finish your car in under ten minutes, a first-rate deal.

I was pondering over the wise words of Gary Vaynerchuk, of how he is constantly trying to put himself out of business. Which got me thinking about what could be done to put an oil change company out of business, other than removal of their independence on fossil fuels for vehicles. Oil changes being a quasi-utility, makes it a very secure business or so you would think. I'm sure that's what the taxicab companies thought before the arrival of Uber and Lyft.

Part of the reason I became self-employed was to be able to engulf my entire life in my business. The closest I came to this was when I was thirteen running an Earthbound fan page called Giygas.net/Mother2.net, which had a very strong following. After that, my life was immersed in baseball and only baseball. I identified with both of these things because I had ownership over both and they were an integral part of me. Quickly after the purchase of Quick Change, I realized that there was only so much I could do to further the business. There are only so many people on social media, within a reasonable demographic in Harrisburg to get an oil change.

    I immediately broke down the factors of the oil change business and looked for opportunities to reach out to the D.I.Y.ers. I contacted my distributors to see what lines of product move the most, that was when Service Champ provided me with a product popularity listing. Based on the categorization of what the distributors were sending out to most of their vendors, such as myself, I immediately started posting oil filters on Amazon and eBay in packs of six. Due to the fact that I get wholesale pricing from the manufacturer, whether it is Mobil1 or Castrol, I had the foresight to list a lot of these products on Amazon and eBay for the first time. Oil filters are not traditionally sold online, but I had the advantage of having the numbers directly from the manufacturers of what products move faster than others, simple matter of supply and demand. The revenues were so immediate that I established a new business overnight centered completely around the demand and distribution of oil change products, aptly named Oleum Oils.

Sold (last 60 days)

Listed	38
Sold	39
Amount	$3,161.61

Payments (last 60 days)

Received	$3,064.64
Not received	$96.97
Total sales:	$3,161.61

eBay Sales

Sales Summary
Last updated 5/9/16 9:54:40 AM PDT

	Ordered product sales	Units
Today	$0.00	0
7 Days	$65.46	3
15 Days	$169.90	7
30 Days	$490.25	16

Amazon Sales

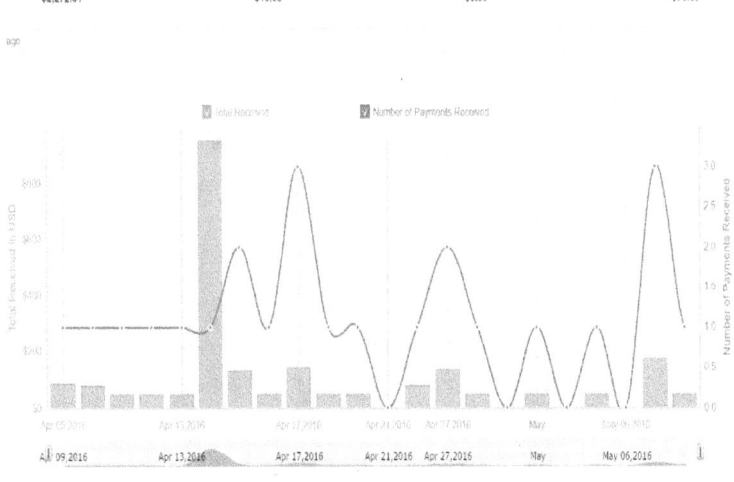

Oleum Oil WooCommerce Sales OleumOils.com

Continuing on this idea spree of "How am I going to put myself out of business?" I thought about trying to create the "Uber of oil changes," but it wouldn't be very practical, and ideas are shit — execution is everything. As far as ideas go, my next brilliant one was an app where you could hire a lube tech to come do your oil change while you're at work or even while you're at home. Not only that, but if you could also negotiate a price over the app then that would be an excellent program that could shake up the oil change industry.

As far as ingenious ideas, I am trying a more practical approach with my latest project OilChangeCase.com. I will write in more depth about this later but essentially, it's a kit for the D.I.Y.ers. If you're a business owner, it's important to think about how you can put yourself out of business. As well as various ways to innovate your own industry. I am constantly looking at every aspect of the industry looking for ways to improve it in any way I can.

Amerilube 10 Minute Oil Change in Dillsburg, Pennsylvania: No Money

Amerilube was number three. Amerilube is now the third business I have owned, which I was able to acquire for little to no money with this particular instance being no money.

Amerilube 10 Minute Oil Change in Dillsburg, PA

I am a big proponent of business ownership, self-employment, and entrepreneurship. I strongly disagree when people say "someone has to be the ditch digger." I myself have a dozen W2 employees, but if the social norm were 1099 Independent Contractors then I wouldn't have any problem with that either. The reality of the world is, there are people out there either not suited for self-employment, or that just have no real interest in it. I think it is often discouraged more than it should be, but there is certainly no shortage of W2 employees out there in the market.

To bring anyone up to speed who isn't familiar with my back story—I am the son of a Greek Family from Kalamata on the Peloponnese side of Greece. My family built a business in Maine that started from nothing and eventually became something really special and proprietary. I went to college in Maryland, predominantly only caring about baseball, of which I was on a scholarship for. I graduated in 2010 and continued on to play professional baseball. My baseball journey came to an abrupt halt due to a significant injury to my labrum and rotator cuff. It wasn't easy finding a job in 2010, but thanks to a coincidence where a bank manager was from Maine, "Us Main-ahs stick to-get-thah.," I was hired to work for TD Bank. I worked in finance for four years including working for TD Ameritrade, Merrill Lynch, and T. Rowe Price. In the winter of 2014, I discovered a classifieds website that listed businesses for sale. Turns out, back in the day you could only really find a centralized database of businesses for sale in the Wall Street Journal on Thursdays. Obviously thanks to the internet, you can now find businesses for sale on sites like eBay and Craigslist, but who can you really trust? Fortunately, BizBuySell created a genuine system that allowed protection for both the buyers and the sellers of businesses.

I knew I had to become self-employed or else I would have gone insane working for someone else my entire life, and one virtue I truly lack is patience. I decided I would buy an existing business and run it for awhile, before making the switch to full-time self-employment.

When I started looking for quick lubes for sale I was hesitant to get into that particular industry because that is the business my father built from the ground up back home in Maine. I was worried that whatever success I would achieve in this industry would be attributed to being my father's son. I ultimately bought the business behind my family's back, without any prior knowledge of what I was attempting to do. Eventually, any worries and apprehension I had about what other people thought passed fairly quickly because shortly thereafter everything else fell into place. In light of this, I have a much better outlook on and understanding of life in general.

Owner or Seller Financing

Owner or seller financing is one of the most common ways of purchasing an existing business and typically it is a good sign when an owner is offering seller financing to sell their business. This is how I was able to purchase Quick Change Inc., the Quick Lube I currently own and operate in Harrisburg, Pennsylvania. This is also sort of how I was able to procure Amerilube, the second location that I am opening in July.

Business Name History

Name	Name Type
The Kapothanasis Group Inc	Current Name

Business Entity Details		Officers
Name	The Kapothanasis Group Inc	
Entity Number	4360417	
Entity Type	Business Corporation	
Status	Active	
Citizenship	Foreign	
Entity Creation Date	06/05/2015	
Effective Date	05/20/2015	
State Of Inc	MD	
Address	2720 Walnut St Harrisburg PA 17103	

[Form: Pennsylvania Department of State, Bureau of Corporations and Charitable Organizations — Application for Certificate of Authority (15 Pa.C.S.), filed JUN 05 2015, Entity # 4360417. Foreign Business Corporation (§ 4124). Name: Constantine Kapotharasis, 7015 Folded Palm, Columbia MD 21045. Corporation name: The Kapotharasis Group Inc. Name adopted for use in Commonwealth: Quick Change Oil. Fictitious name: Quick Change Oil. Jurisdiction: Maryland. Principal office: 7015 Folded Palm, Columbia, MD 21045. Commercial Registered Office Provider: 2720 Walnut St, Harrisburg, PA 17103, Dauphin County.]

Banks currently aren't lending to those trying to purchase a business and to even begin to encourage them to look at your own deal, you better have two or three times the collateral with regards to the potential mortgage amount. Irregardless of whether the business is extremely profitable or not and just because they might take a look at your business loan request doesn't necessarily mean they will approve it. Even non-bank lenders aren't lending for the purchase of the business unless the business comes with a substantial amount of real estate, after which they will only fund it depending on a small loan-to-current-value of the real estate. That leaves two options for most of us wanting to purchase the business of our dreams:

- Friends, as well as family, or what a few call friends, loved ones or even fools. Nevertheless, unless you possess a rich wealthy Uncle, most of your family and friends are also dealing with financing restraints and either won't or cannot help you fund a big purchase like that of purchasing a business.
- Owner funding is when the current owner from the business is prepared to sell it to you on terms, thus meaning these people - not the financial institution - hold onto the actual note.

This is what we should and will discuss right here and now, as this may truly be the only method left to buy a business today. Owner financing may benefit the purchaser, you, in many ways:

- It's easier to be eligible for as you don't need to jump through all of the hoops that banking institutions or lenders can make you jump through, such as income analysis, property value determinations, debt-to-income ratios, individual financial statements, and so on and so forth.
- It tends to offer better terms compared to what most banks will offer you—thus, saving the brand-new owner and the purchaser, each time and money—as well as, substantially less in relation to reporting, ongoing monetary statements and taxes returns. As well as, less covenants.
- More than simply financing, since the present owner still has a stake in the actual business's success, they'll provide invaluable assistance and advice well into the future.
- Plus, if the current business proprietor believes in the commercial and you can encourage them to believe in you, then this will be hands down a smart choice for the proprietor. If they wait without giving an excellent reason, that might be considered a red flag to you as it can also show that the present owner does not have confidence in the long-term viability of the business. Their hesitation proves they believe something is incorrect or in decline.

How I Bought Amerilube for Zero Dollars
The Opportunities are Clearly Out There

So after I took over one hundred percent control of Quick Change for less than fifteen grand using only credit card cash advances, it made a lot of people say that it was just lucky timing. Then, I was able to buy a Vape Shop for less than five grand — again, I was apparently lucky. BUT the fact that I was able to take over an existing business for the third time in a twelve-month time period, and one that was within the industry that I was already in leads me to believe that it was more than just luck. I believe that because I strongly believe that this is something that anyone can do.

The Amerilube Story

Amerilube was a quick lube founded in 2001, that had run uninterrupted for fifteen years operating under two different owners. The original owner grew the business first before handing it over to Mr. Belize. Mr. Belize is a pseudonym, and not his actual name.

Mr. Belize, much like myself, was in the financial industry before buying Amerilube from its founder. Amerilube's books were very similar to Quick Change's. Amerilube had a peak of revenue much higher than that of Quick Change and its drop-in revenue wasn't as significant. However, Amerilube's online presence was nonexistent. They had no website whatsoever, not even a Facebook page. Amerilube was at the whim of their competitors' negative reviews, as well as their history of bad service that it had provided for the majority of a prior three-year period.

Amerilube appeared on my radar in the summer of 2015, not too long after I took over Quick Change. I immediately reached out to the listing broker for more information on the business. When you try to buy a business, nine out of ten times you will deal with a business broker. I have written about this previously, as well. Although, I would not actually speak with Mr. Belize until nearly a year later.

The listing broker was Cindy Olweiler of MCA Brokers, which is her real name because I have no problem disclosing it due to the fact that dealing with her was a real nightmare. MCA Brokers is a combo realty group, which in my opinion is the worst kind. If you're a business broker then sell businesses, and if you're a commercial agent, then you should only sell and buy commercial. Lastly, if you're a residential agent then stick to residential. Realtors in general annoy me, but business brokers who have a side realty business are even worse because typically they don't know how to properly value a business. They tend to take everything personally because real estate, for whatever reason, is a more emotional business.

I first e-mailed Cindy in August of 2015, three months after taking over Quick Change. Originally, Mr. Belize was only interested in selling the business if the property went along with the business — his valuation of both the business and the real estate somehow came to $450,000 dollars. Mr. Belize was planning to move to Belize permanently and leave America behind. See what I did there? It made me smile, hope I made you smile, too.

With only one tax return under The Kapothanasis Group Inc.'s belt, I wouldn't be able to qualify for traditional funding. I did however, have the books to the business and knew Mr. Belize was in trouble. I pursued the business with determination. I wasn't going to be able to buy the building but I wanted the business at all costs.

Cindy stopped answering my questions when a so-called potential buyer came along and said that they wanted to put a restaurant on top of Amerilube. When I heard this news, I was devastated. It was a fantastic location for a fast food restaurant, so it didn't surprise me in the least. I called my Dad to let him know what happened. The conversation with my Dad was as follows:

Costa: "Dad, it's over, I'm not going to be able to get the quick lube in Dillsburg."

Dad: "Why?"

Costa: "There is a restaurant investor that wants to knock it down and put in a fast food joint."

Dad: "Like fuck there is!"

Costa: "What do you mean?"

Dad: "There is NO restaurant going there. Trust me!"

Costa: "O.K. Dad. Thanks"

So, I pushed forward and later received an e-mail from Cindy, as shown below:

From: Cindy Olweiler [mail to: Cindy@mcabizbrokers.com]
Received: August 23rd, 2015
To: Me

To address your questions...

1) I will ask the seller.

2) I will ask the seller.

3) Although you would be purchasing the business name, you can change it if you wish.

4) I will check, but those types of contracts don't necessarily transfer with the sale of a business.

Not sure which comps you are looking at for the area, but the $400,000 asking price is in line...the property appraised for $450,000 a few years ago, ...and there is also a value of the business and equipment. There is very little negotiation room, if any, with the pricing. The building right next door, which is comparable in size, is currently listed at $795,000.

Cindy

Cindy L. Miller-Olweiler
Senior Broker Associate
MCA Business Brokers & Realty
Cell: (717) 304–9787
www.MCABizBrokers.com

From: Costa Kapothanasis [mail to: CostaKapothanasis@gmail.com]

Sent: Sunday, August 23rd, 2015 3:35 PM

To: Cindy Olweiler

Subject: Re: Dillsburg Quick Lube

Do you have the vendors name for who collects his used oil?

From: Costa Kapothanasis [mail to: CostaKapothanasis@gmail.com]
Sent: Sunday, August 23rd, 2015

To: Cindy Olweiler

I can share my comps and numbers for sure, that is not a problem. 450k, even with the new Advanced Auto and even if it were a drive-by appraisal is more than the lot is worth. He bought the place for 300K in 2008, just barely after the most overvalued real estate market in U.S. history.

Regardless if he is stuck on that price, that is his prerogative for sure, and the intangibles in the location, for me at least make me willing to pursue it at that asking cost, but it would be nice if he were a little more realistic about a business that has consistently been losing money and a lot that is most likely overvalued.

Let me know when you get those answers because if he is paying anything over five dollars per gallon for oil he is paying too much and that is a cost right there that would make the business profitable again.

Thanks,
Costa

This is where things started going south in the e-mails. The e-mail is as follows:

From: Costa Kapothanasis [mail to: CostaKapothanasis@gmail.com]

Sent: Sunday, August 23rd, 2015

To: Cindy Olweiler

Do you have the vendors name for who collects his used oil?

Who is his oil distributor, are they in a contract? And for conventional 5W20 what does he currently pay per gallon?

Is Amerilube proprietary? Is there anything stopping me from changing and overhauling the marketing and branding after purchase?

Are there any long-term contracts? Merchant Services? Uniforms? Filters? Etc.

Knowing the oil price per gallon is probably the most important aspect because of the bulk oil prices I get, it's possible I can make the company profitable based on that alone.

Could you also tell me more about the valuation? All the comparables in the area would suggest this asking price is nearly 10K too much.

Thanks,
Costa

From: Cindy Olweiler [mail to: Cindy@mcabizbrokers.com]

Received: Sunday, August 23rd, 2015

To: Me

To be honest, if you are going to offer considerably less, there is no reason to get the questions answered. What the buyer paid to purchase the business and the real estate (which were purchased separately, so not at the amount that you noted) has nothing to do with the current value. There is another buyer who has been at the location with his contractor already and is going to be writing an offer. And there is a second buyer who is meeting at the location this coming week. They are both interested in the real estate only, so the business equipment would be sold separately.

If you are now in a position where you feel confident that you will be able to provide the required down payment, then you may want to consider writing an offer. Please advise if you will have access to provide a fifteen to twenty percent down payment.

Take care,

Cindy

In her e-mail, she was out of line. She is a broker, it is not her place to decide whether or not answering my questions is a waste of time. As the broker, she is paid to answer those questions regardless of the offer. This is where the emotional nature of real estate seems to cloud the dual broker's minds. She is clearly offended at this point and because of this she doesn't want to perform the duties of her job. It is not her place to choose when and when not to answer a buyer's questions. My response to her out of line e-mail is as follows:

From: Costa Kapothanasis [mail to: CostaKapothanasis@gmail.com]
Sent: Sunday, August 23rd, 2015

To: Cindy Olweiler

I cannot write an offer in good faith without those questions answered.

Thanks, Costa

From: Cindy Olweiler [mail to: Cindy@mcabizbrokers.com]

Received: Monday, August 24th, 2015

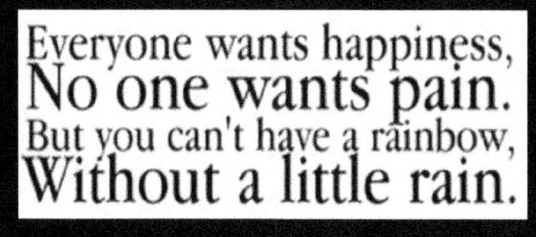

To: Me

I will get the questions answered for you only if you now have the down payment money. However, the seller is going to want to have confirmation that you have found a way to come up with fifteen to twenty percent down payment. Last time we talked, that wasn't the case, so I need an update to know if that has changed

She was out of line yet again. It is also not a broker's place to question whether I have the funding or not. If I am going to submit a formal offer, you can assume that I have the funding for the transaction. This isn't real estate, I don't need to be prequalified. This is business and I am no amateur. I have bought a business before with only a bill of sale on a bar napkin in Fed Hill Baltimore, MD. At this point, I am done with her. I had reached out to my friends in commercial real estate and I had even consulted my dad who is also familiar with these matters and they all told me to just walk away. But what about my oil empire?!

This was a tough call. I was already speaking to people about how it is important to never get emotionally attached to a business, but I wanted Amerilube SO BAD. It was difficult to walk away, but I took a step back and took a good look at the situation. I looked at it from the lens of a rational and objective business person, but unfortunately everything said walk away. My heart said don't give up, while my head said walk away. So, I did just that.

My Dad actually called what happened next way before I did, he said that she would be back eventually, and that they weren't getting a restaurant in there. He then told me to be patient, which wasn't my forte.

> From: Cindy Olweiler [mail to: Cindy@mcabizbrokers.com]
>
> Received: Friday, September 18th, 2015
>
> To: Me
>
> Hello,
>
> Costa……the seller has asked me to come back to you to see if you still have interest in this property. The other buyer has decided not to move forward based on the costs of renovating the building to become a restaurant. The answers to your remaining questions are below.
>
>> Who is his oil distributor, are they in a contract? And for conventional 5W20 what does he currently pay per gallon? PPC Lubricants and he pays $6.15 per gallon.
>>
>> Are there any long-term contracts? Merchant Services? Uniforms? Filters? No long-term contracts.
>
> Cindy
>
> Cindy L. Miller-Olweiler
> Senior Broker Associate
> MCA Business Brokers & Realty
> Cell: (717) 304-9787
>
> www.MCABizBrokers.com

From: Costa Kapothanasis [mail to: CostaKapothanasis@gmail.com]

Sent: Tuesday, November 3rd, 2015

To: Cindy Olweiler

Is the business still for sale and are the doors still open?

From: Cindy Olweiler [mail to: Cindy@mcabizbrokers.com]

Sent: Tuesday, November 3rd, 2015

To: Me

Yes, to both questions. The seller is also open to leasing the real estate to the buyer of the business.

Cindy

Cindy L. Miller-Olweiler
Senior Broker Associate
MCA Business Brokers & Realty
Cell: (717) 304–9787

www.MCABizBrokers.com

From: Costa Kapothanasis [mail to: CostaKapothanasis@gmail.com]

Sent: Tuesday, November 3rd, 2015 5:31 PM

To: Cindy Olweiler

I am assuming he wants the full 50K in cash for the business in that particular situation?

From: Cindy Olweiler [mail to: Cindy@mcabizbrokers.com]

Sent: Tuesday, November 3rd, 2015

To: Me

He does not want to hold a seller note if that is what you are asking. He may be persuaded to hold 10K or so, but I would have to confirm that.

From: Costa Kapothanasis [mail to: CostaKapothanasis@gmail.com]

Sent: Tuesday, November 3rd, 2015 5:44 PM

To: Cindy Olweiler

O.K., I am going to contact my friend at NAI CIR to run some numbers, and I am going to take a look at what cash I can put together and I will put together a formal offer.

Thanks,

Costa

From: Cindy Olweiler [mail to: Cindy@mcabizbrokers.com]

Sent: Tuesday, November 3rd, 2015

To: Me

Will you be writing up the offer through MCA or will your attorney be doing that for you?

From: Costa Kapothanasis [mail to: CostaKapothanasis@gmail.com]

Sent: Tuesday, November 3rd, 2015 5:57 PM

To: Cindy Olweiler

I will use my attorney that I've used to purchase all my existing businesses through.

From: Cindy Olweiler [mail to: Cindy@mcabizbrokers.com]

Sent: Tuesday, November 3rd, 2015

To: Me

Sounds good. Please let me know if I can answer any other questions for you.

                                                      Cindy

For the purposes of not boring you to death and expediency I am going to just paste in plain text the remaining correspondence as follows:

To Cindy:

I went to the business today and pretended to be a customer. I accidentally went in the exit which ended up being fortunate because I didn't drive over the bell trip in the parking lot. I walked in and one of the employees was passed out in the chair snoring away. Regardless that the location is good, both the building and business have obviously been severely neglected. Despite this, I want to put in an offer which I will be writing up tomorrow. The valuation method I use is a combination of multiple earnings and a capitalization rate. I am interested in buying the property but my corporation won't have two-year tax returns until August of 2016, so I intend to ask for a lease to buy intent situation. I'll have the offer in your inbox by tomorrow night.

To Cindy:

Cindy,

Attached is the formal offer letter. It's a standard purchase agreement letter, I have left some date spots open if the buyer chooses to accept it.

Like I said yesterday, I used a Multiple of Earnings and Capitalization Rate calculation to create a valuation of the business. Solely on calculations alone the business is worth a hair under $14,000 dollars, and that was based on the 2009–2012 numbers. I didn't bother doing the valuation on the updated numbers because it is most likely not worth anything right now, especially with that hugely accelerated depreciation of sales year after year. It is more than just a trend at this point, it is a strong trend.

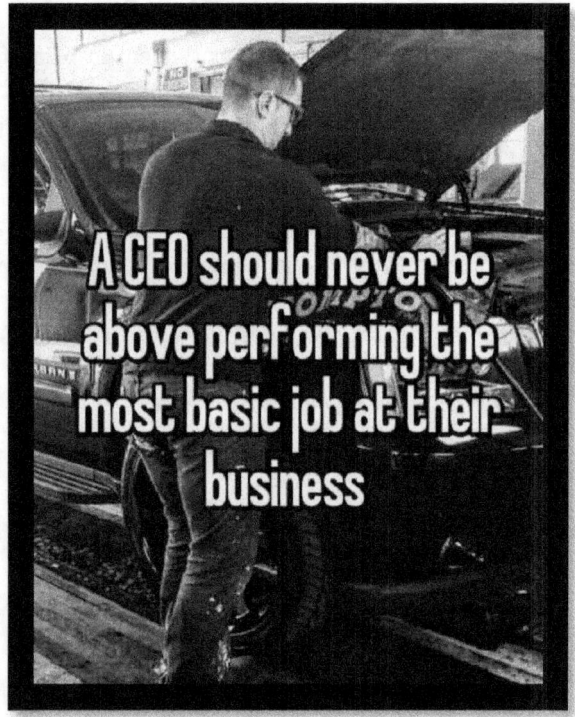

That being said, the contents of my offer is a $28,000 dollar cash purchase at closing with a $10,000 held seller note amortized over five years at six percent. In all likelihood, it would get paid back within the first couple years, but in order to revitalize this business I need to retain as much cash flow early on as possible. This cash offer is two times more than what the company was worth in 2012, and the total package is three times that amount.

My projected numbers to bring this business back to life also require an $1,800 monthly lease, which coincidentally is what he paid himself as rent in 2014.

Please pass this along to the buyer and let me know how he feels about this offer.

Also, if he doesn't already know, one of his garage doors is broken. If he accepts my offer, I will pay for the repair myself.

Thanks,

Costa

From: Cindy Olweiler [mail to: Cindy@mcabizbrokers.com]

Sent: Wednesday, November 11th, 2015

To: Me

The seller is unrealistic in what he feels he should receive for a monthly rental. I will be in touch later today.

Cindy

To Cindy:

The most I could do is $2,200 in rent, plus he would get $190 a month from the $10,000 note.

He should understand that this is all based on math from the projected revenues of 2014. He won't be getting a check that can be cashed if he goes any higher.

A bomb is dropped for a second time as follows:

From: Cindy Olweiler [mail to: Cindy@mcabizbrokers.com]

Sent: Wednesday, November 11th, 2015

To: Me

Unfortunately, the seller is not able to accept your offer. His wife has already accepted a job in Maryland, and the seller is anxious to sell the real estate and move as soon as possible. His mortgage payment is considerably higher than any lease payment that he would be able to obtain, so he has elected to drop the price of the real estate to $300,000 which will include the business assets.

I appreciate your offer to purchase the business…and am sorry that it will not work out. If you have any interest in purchasing the real estate and business assets for $300,000, please let me know.

Take care.

Cindy

Cindy L. Miller-Olweiler
Senior Broker Associate
MCA Business Brokers & Realty
Cell: (717) 304–9787

www.MCABizBrokers.com

My last-ditch Hail Mary, is as follows:

To Cindy:

Cindy,

Thanks for keeping in touch. This is obviously very disappointing. I appreciate all the work you have been doing during this process. I am going to try to stay optimistic and hope that the buyer comes to his senses. The mortgage he took out in 2009 was 290K so even at a fifteen-year mortgage with rates how they were then, I don't see how his mortgage could possibly be more than $2,200 a month, so I don't think he is being forthcoming with you.

If he wants to go through with it, I have $30,000 in cash in an account that will be immediately available. I can even bump it up to 35K off the bat and keep the 10K seller held note for five years. I have to stick with $2000 a month otherwise the place simply won't make enough money to pay for itself.

Thanks,

Costa

To Cindy:

What exactly does he need for a lease number to match his loan payment? It really would be such a waste for this business to go under when it is just an active owner and operator away from that $350,000 in revenue year it had in 2009.

To Cindy:

Okay, that is fine. It's confusing and doesn't make any sense to me but if that is what the current situation is there is no changing that then.

In any case if the seller has trouble unloading everything please reach out.

And just like that all replies and correspondence stopped.

What happens next? What now? you may ask. This is the situation where being unemotional about business is extremely helpful. It was disappointing but I needed to move forward. I am building a legacy and this would be just one stop on a very long journey.

However, I couldn't shake the location. I drove by that location every single day, even after it closed down. There was no activity whatsoever. It was tough to stare at the empty property day after day. Every time I drove by I thought about how I could be turning that store into a gem. Every day I drove by the property and nothing changed, until one day it did when a white piece of paper went up on the door. Damn, O.K. now I was curious. I decided to go read the paper on the door. I drove down to the store and read the sign. Damn, someone bought it. An Ian Fleming, another pseudonym and not his real name, bought it. Hmmm...lucky guy? Maybe but depends on what he bought it for, I thought to myself. O.K. well out of curiosity, let me write his number down. I continued to drive by for three months and nothing changed. I was unsure of what was happening with the property because there was no construction and there was no activity. I decided to call the number one day, the conversation went as follows:

Ian Fleming: "Hello, this is Ian Fleming."

Costa: "Hello, I drive by Amerilube every single day and I was just wondering what your plans are for it?"

A fortuitous change of events had occurred, Mr. Fleming had bought the property with his friend and partner in the hopes of building a Taco Bell on it. Mr. Belize had moved to Belize and flat out abandoned the business. The employees didn't find out until the day Mr. Fleming had bought the building. Kind of a dick move, if you ask me.

I had all the leverage in the world at this point. I knew how much the building sold for, the ceiling, and I knew the mortgage price that the new investors would be paying. I also knew that no fast food restaurant would be going into that location. I had it on good authority from a reliable source, that a fast food chain was not going into this location. Now I never reveal my sources, but my source knew beyond a shadow of a doubt with one hundred percent certainty that a fast food chain was not going in that location.

I was one hundred percent emotionally unattached to that property. It had been dangled in front of me so many times that I no longer had expectations. I asked Mr. Fleming if I could audit the inventory left behind by Mr. Belize and he agreed to let me. Damn, I was still in disbelief that Mr. Belize had abandoned the whole business and just left it behind so easily. A business that I had previously offered him 50K in cash for five months earlier. The doors could have been opened the same day as my offer and business could have resumed as usual.

I wrote up my offer to Mr. Fleming, which essentially was to sign the lease and sell some of the existing inventory to have the proceeds go to him and his partner. However, anything not bolted down to the floor would then belong to me. He had to put up a front, but he did mention there was a potential restaurant buyer. Fortunately for me, thanks to my reliable source I knew there wasn't one. So, I held firm on my offer but mentioned I could sign a lease within the week.

It took three days for him to agree and say "O.K., let's do this." Wow! I was in shock. I now had officially bought three separate businesses with little to no money — Amerilube, which was the best of the three P&L wise with literally ZERO money. You can too!

Payless Express 10 Minute Oil Change in Chicago, IL

Payless Express Oil Change is truly a story of leverage if I have ever heard one. Payless was an old quick lube situated in a suburb of Chicago that had a loyal following and a twenty plus year history. The business sale price was listed at $149,000 dollars, money that I didn't exactly have, but I still requested the books on it anyway because I was looking to grow my business quickly, with or without money.

I flew out to Chicago to meet with the owner who was a seemingly nice enough guy. He had originally purchased it from the founder of the business sometime in the 2000's. I sat in the parking lot for an extensive amount of hours just to observe the daily business operations. The set-up wasn't ideal, as it was situated in an Auto Mall with dozens of other Auto Shops surrounding it. While it was the only quick lube, it wasn't the only business that did oil changes.

Eventually, I went in and met with the owner to talk to him about the business and the numbers and finances of the business. The numbers include cash flow, net-income, gross income, profit and loss, sales, price point, gross margin, as well as take of inventory. After reviewing the numbers with the owner, the numbers themselves were very good, but I was unsure of the reliability of them due to the haphazard formatting of the P&L, profit and loss. The saving grace was that the two existing employees had tenure and had both worked there for an excess of twenty years. Their combined knowledge, experience, and expertise, as well as their accumulative history of the business was greatly appreciated. After a full day of due diligence, I flew back to Baltimore with a great deal to think about.

Shortly thereafter, the owner called me and expressed with great urgency and the need to move quickly. For this reason he said he was dropping the price down to $49,000. This price was more in my wheelhouse now. Anytime I'm able to buy a business whose net-income is at least six-figures and purchase it for under $50,000, it's always a good deal, and a great day. After our conversation, I flew back out to Chicago to meet with the landlord and the owner of the business again. During the meeting this is when I found out the revealing details which gave me exactly the leverage that I needed to steal this business from the owner. Due to the circumstances, I found out about, the owner of the business was being pushed out one way or another. He was going to be pushed out of the business irregardless, and wind up with either a little bit of money to profit in his pocket or none at all. This is where research and knowledge are extremely important. It pays to always do your due diligence when thinking about purchasing a business. In situations like this where business owners are being forced out of their companies, their only options are liquidation or abandonment. Understanding how to price inventory while simultaneously knowing how difficult it is to unload that inventory is key leverage. The owner had previously told me if I didn't make a deal he was going to back up the u-haul, throw the equipment in the truck, and try to sell it on eBay. Although, little did he know that I knew this wasn't going to happen for a myriad of reasons, including an emotional attachment to his existing employees.

On the way to the airport to fly home I decided to text the owner saying "I would buy the business for $5,000 all cash, no questions asked, contingent on an acceptable lease with the landlord." He proceeded to ask me if I could make a better offer or go any higher, because he tried to assure me that he couldn't let the business go and sell it for such a low amount. I replied that "I was sorry, and that was the best that I could offer given the current circumstances." In that moment, I was boarding the plane through the boarding gate I received the text message "Deal." from the owner.

These situations are out there! I have armed you with the tools, knowledge, and know-how that you need to find them. I have done it personally now three times, without needing any kind of exterior help, which means that you can do it too!

www.ingramcontent.com/pod-product-compliance
Lightning Source LLC
Chambersburg PA
CBHW070046210526
45170CB00012B/604